D0475924

# AT NIGHT

# AT NIGHT

A.Q.

First published in 2014 by Old Street Publishing Ltd,
8 Sulivan Road, London
www.oldstreetpublishing.co.uk

ISBN 978 1 908699 84 8

10 9 8 7 6 5 4 3 2 1

A CIP catalogue record for this title is available from the British Library.

Printed and bound by CPI Group (UK) Ltd, Croydon, CR0 4YY

With thanks to Richard Freeston, Clement Dexter,
Carole Ponniah, Mengwei Hu, James Dexter
and Richard Parsons

# CONTENTS

# AT NIGHT

# I

# TURN OFF ALL ELECTRONIC DEVICES

This is a precondition of any true appreciation of the night. Please do not fritter away the hours of darkness looking at your phone, playing cards with robots on the internet, pressing buttons on an e-reader, or watching television. The night is, or should be, sacred. As Louis Armstrong sang:

> The bright blessed day
> The dark sacred night!

Yes, it's a wonderful world. The night, in which all the world's sobs are hushed and all of history's torments soothed. Do you wish to pollute it with the jangling noise of Sonic the Hedgehog as he collects the rings that mean so much to him? When, instead, you could think, speculate, create? Do you really intend to waste that time making avatars run futilely against walls?

Please turn from all televisions and screens. If you are perusing this on an e-reader, put it aside. Make a small bonfire, and place the e-reader on it.

Now kindle it.

# II

# WELCOME THE SUNSET

What is a sunset? A spectacle for lovers? An adjunct to a Caribbean holiday? Or is it something more?

Perhaps a sunset as a gateway. Once we have passed through it, life takes on a more serious cast. All day, we have feinted with existence; after sunset, the contest is in earnest and the swords are untipped. A transition has taken place: from the mundane to the mysterious, from prose to poetry, temporal to timeless. We are, as night progresses, more and more alone, less and less served by civilization. Archaic fears rise within us. Rabbits give way to badgers, snails to slugs. And they may be very large slugs; especially on that Caribbean island.

Night, like a forgotten library, has tracts unexplored. Who is to say, in fact, that the night will ever end? This was the philosophy of David Hume. Just because the sun rose yesterday does not mean it will tomorrow, and to assert its inevitable re-appearance is to fall into the largest and most open trap of inductive reasoning. Karl Popper made the same point, and Bertrand Russell too. These were stern men who, when they went to bed at night, disdained to set their alarm clocks; and who, when morning did arrive, looked in vain in their larders for bacon and eggs, since, secure in their positivism, they had failed to buy any the previous day.

Welcome the sunset; but be aware, it may be your last.

# ENJOY THE SILENCE

Night silence is more than the mere absence of diurnal noise. Silence at night allows a new soundscape to emerge. Have you ever heard a rat plop gently into a garden pond at 3am? No? You must try it sometime. It is a subtle, thoughtful splash; a rat-meditation, almost.

A cat swishes through grasses, periodically stopping and listening. Crickets chirp. Frogs croak. Bats squeak. A fox barks. A tawny owl hoots. A distant motorbike clears its throat. Nature abhors a vacuum, just as a student abhors a vacuum cleaner.

In the house, ancient heating pipes click as they expand; rain percolates under tiles and gathers in pudgy drips on the bathroom ceiling. A heavy desk minutely settles on its fat ankles, children respire, a mouse gnaws behind a wall. There are five clocks, all with a different tock, all fluttering after one another in a frantic attempt to catch up. And the unidentifiable sounds: a periodic booming thud; a trickling, a scraping, a rustling, a slithering; a dipping hum; a sussuration.

You may say here, or here, is silence, here is nothingness; but listen carefully and there will always be something delicate, elusive and faint, something new underneath, some layer of tiny violence.

# IV

# VIEW THE MOON

The sun is a dog, the moon a cat. The sun has his regular walks in the day, the moon her irregular prowls in the night. Everyone knows through which windows and curtains the sun will cock a leg. But the moon: where and when will she arch her gleaming back? Only she and astronomers know.

There is a tale about an old Chinese man who was invited to a moon-viewing party. It used to be traditional for Chinese people to view the moon during the mid-Autumn festival, at which time they would eat moon-cakes, drink rice wine and enjoy the warmth of the night. The moon, as we know, keeps one face turned to the earth, and the Chinese swear they can see, in that constant face, the shape of a jade rabbit grinding something with a mortar and pestle. Anyway, the man was just leaving the house for the party when a servant ran up and told him that this year there would be a special treat: loudspeakers would play a recorded version of Beethoven's 'Moonlight Serenade' to entertain the guests. The old man immediately cancelled his plans and returned to the house.

Sometimes even the greatest art is like a scab on the skin of life.

# V

# VIEW THE VARIOUS
# FULL MOONS

At certain times of the year the full moon takes on a particular cast. Many people are familiar, for instance, with the 'Hunter's moon' of October. This full moon is large and reddish, and guides night-time sportsmen, lustful for blood, to their quarry. There is also the 'Harvest moon' of September, by the light of which grain is gathered home and folk are fed. Other full moons include the 'Milk moon' of May, a moon of a palish and pearlescent cast, associated by tradition with lovelorn ladies, the 'Hare moon' of March, under whose magical beams hares come out to box and primp themselves, and the 'Hunger moon' of January, a wolfish season when the moon itself looks temptingly edible.

In reality all these moons are exactly the same, since the moon is always full when the ecliptic longitude of the sun and the moon are 180 degrees apart: there is very little difference in size, colour or any other factor. These are all a matter of the imagination. But ask yourself: in which world would you rather live? One which spoke of languishing ladies, boxing hares and sexually hepped-up gunmen splashing in fens, or one in which the appearance of the full moon is predicted by the formula $D = 20.362955 + 29.530588861 \times N + 102.026 \times 10^{12} \times N^2$?

# VI

# LISTEN TO CLOCKS AND BELLS IN THE CITY

'The dead of night' is an evocative phrase. There is a moment in the deepest depths of the night – perhaps four o'clock on a winter's morn – when time seems to have stopped, as a ball thrown into the air pauses at the tip of its parabola before making the lazy decision to return to earth. There is a watchful, listening silence. Then from this most meditative of silences, sounds emerge: the clocks and bells of the city.

There is the bell of the guildhall marking the half and quarter hours with ghastly clangs. The cathedral tolls two, three, four, with the regularity of a curate's subscription to the *Church Times*. The jewellers' clock, with its slick whirr of brass cogs and tinny bash of bells. 'Do not ask for whom the bell tolls; it tolls for thee.' And if thou art the only person awake, it doth indeed toll for thee.

What truly connects you to the past? Precious little. The high street is a trashy parade of cloned modernity. Your neighbours have the bad taste to be quite young. Even your geriatrician is only twenty-six. Only the bells, linking you to generations now gone: the bells are their wedding bells, funeral bells, bells of plague, bells of fire. In the dead of night, the dead.

# VII

# DISPOSE OF A CORPSE

There are manuals aplenty that detail the proper method for doing this. They are called 'crime fiction'. The idea of crime fiction is to present murder, torture and rape in such a way that it can be enjoyed comfortably in an armchair in front of a roaring fire by persons who would shriek with horror at the sight of a spider. According to these manuals, night is a valuable ally in most body disposal methods.

If one has nothing to dispose of, not having murdered anyone, one may *pretend* to dispose of a corpse. This will lead the neighbours to think they have discovered a real murderer living next door to them: and indeed, it is a strange fact that most murders are committed by people with neighbours. Your neighbours will very likely be devotees of the most garishly pornographic crime fiction, and will think themselves thrillingly precipitated into a real-life version of their borrowed fancies.

Around eleven, when they are preparing for bed, begin digging a large hole in your garden. Cover it with a tarpaulin and repeat the following night until you are sure of being watched. Then manhandle a large, plastic-wrapped, cylindrical package into the hole. Frenziedly cover it with earth.

While you await the police, practice this statement: 'Yes, I buried a roll of carpet in my back garden. I was merely re-enacting, for my own pleasure, a detective fantasy I saw on television. I find it exciting to do so, and was not aware that it was illegal.'

# VIII

# DRAW UP YOUR OWN ASTROLOGICAL CHART

Many people pooh-pooh astrology as a relic, of an age of ignorance and superstition. This is especially rife among astronomers, who are in some ways the heirs of astrologers. After all, in past ages astronomy and astrology were the same science. A little more understanding and a little less pooh-poohing between the two communities would be nice. After all, if I pooh-pooh you, you feel a reflex urge to pooh-pooh me: and pooh-poohing can lead to wars. It is widely believed that testy cousins exchanging a pooh-pooh was at the root of the 1914-18 conflict, which led to the deaths of 20 million.

Who has the monopoly on truth? A large question. Is it the jolly men with jumpers on television who can recite toothily on the Virgo cluster and Galaxy M22, or the lunatics who delight in exploiting fools by comparing them to heavenly animals?

Perhaps the way to decide is to draw up your own astrological chart. For this, you need a map of the stars. Connect the dots in what seem to you suggestive shapes: animals, people, fruit. Note the month when each shape appears above the horizon, and assign it to people born in that month. For example, you might be born in the House of the Rising Banana. You are therefore delicious, yellow and phallic.

On examining my astrological chart, I find that I fall within the constellation of the Plum Pudding, that is, I am round, spiky and soaked in alcohol. The following month, that of the Leftover Turkey in Foil, is that of my sister Jenna, who is pale, dry and poisonous.

# PLANT VEGETABLES
# UNDER THE FULL MOON

The moon influences the earth in the form of the tides: when it is full, the tides are higher. The moon's phases also influence the behaviours of animals and plants. For example, turtles lay eggs at the full moon, and *habituées* of nightclubs ovulate. Etcetera. However, the full moon may also influence the growth of certain vegetables, so that carrots or potatoes planted around the time of the full moon grow more vigorously. In short, there are waxy potatoes: there are also waxing potatoes.

The Romans knew this: Pliny the Elder informs us that when the full moon appears, 'she replenishes all bodies.' And in the twentieth century, scientists, stern lab-coated men with a cyclotron in one hand and a beaker of anthrax in the other, and no time whatsoever for Pliny the Elder, began to speculate about the reasons for supposed horticultural success during lunar maxima, reasoning that the full moon, having a stronger gravitational pull, might possibly draw up more ground-water to the surface of the earth, thus nourishing plants. Or perhaps the full moon had some influence on the earth's magnetic field, or was responsible for atmospheric ionization helpful to sprouting radishes.

Of course, there is an astrological as well as an astronomical connection. If the moon is in Taurus, some say, runner beans will grow well, and if it is in Scorpio, swede will thrive. Why? No one really knows.

A refuge for the moonstruck of all epochs.

# X

# EXPERIENCE NIGHT-SCENTED FLOWERS

Some flowers bloom at night. They unfold with the silvery kiss of the moon, and, at dawn, shrink back at the rough beard of the sun. They are pollinated by flitting moths or bats, and they give out their most luxurious scents when all other florae are sunk in an envious slumber.

Which species? Well, moonflowers, of course, bloom in the darkling hours. Fairy lilies have an enchanting nocturnal fragrance. The Triple Yellow Devil's Trumpet too: this is a large bush with trumpet-shaped golden flowers up to ten inches long. It is a species of Brugmansia, and releases a sharp, meaty fragrance. All parts of it are poisonous: the flowers, the leaves, the stems and the roots.

Perhaps the most rampantly generous of all night-flowering species is night-flowering jasmine. It is possible to detect this plant hundreds of yards away, its munificence wafted on the night-time breeze, and track it down by smell alone. It might be exuding its cloying sweetness on a wall in some Mediterranean fishing village, or growing with uncontrollable ardour in a Northamptonshire wood in May on the site of a long-collapsed labourer's cottage.

For me, night-flowering jasmine conjures up memories of love so intense as to be painful: though perhaps if that love had been consummated among empty pizza boxes the smell of my neighbour's dustbins would have a similar effect.

# XI

# POE

Who is the true author of the night? Poe. Who invented horror? Poe. Who pioneered the detective tale, set in mud and gloom? Poe. Who, even, in 'The Unparalleled Adventure of One Hans Pfaal', which describes a journey to the moon, invented science fiction, the story of man's flight into the vast blackness of the heavens? Poe. A noun cannot contain this man. There should be a verb, 'to poe'. It would signify contemplation of the night. Night both literal and figurative. 'I poed along the embankment.' 'They left me to poe in my cell.' 'Often have I had good cause to poe on the nature of this man's heart, double-dyed in inky deeds.'

Thanks to Poe, and in particular to his story 'The Mystery of Marie Rogêt', one further development came about: a darkly lascivious interest in the battered and abused corpses of once-beautiful females, which, in direct lineal descent, became the modern televisual preoccupation, firmly settled in every hearth and home, with misogynistic torture, mutilation and death. Poe wrote in his essay 'The Philosophy of Composition' that 'the death of a beautiful woman is unquestionably the most poetical topic in the world.' And with Poe as the true progenitor of the modern blood-bespattered detective drama, we can see Sherlock Holmes, with his gentlemanly conundra about missing jewels or the best way out of a locked room, as a sort of quaint side-street off the main gore-strewn thoroughfare.

Yes, the morbolatrous, woman-haunted, diseased, autumnal and abyssal Mr Poe reaches out to us from beyond the grave and continues to fashion our most delicious nightmares.

# XII

# TRAVERSE A CITY

Next time you pass a public house, look through the window. The revelry seems unconfined, does it not? Everyone is having a grand old time. However, look a little more closely. The clientele form little knots. The knots do not intermingle. The party is in reality a series of solitary groups. People talk and laugh and shout, but they might as well be in a series of separate living rooms. Under the surface, *anomie* extends its creeping tendrils.

Urban life is like that. If you live in a city or town, you live in your house or flat. You go to work, and you frequent certain places in between. These are your knots. At no time do you attempt to embrace your urban existence, to see it whole.

So at night, slide unobtrusively from your home and follow your own footsteps. Traverse your city's boulevards, avenues, side streets and alleyways. Penetrate those areas that you would not normally penetrate: housing estates, railway embankments, waterworks, cemeteries, cathedral cloisters, bus stations, light industrial parks, quays, heaths, woods, golf clubs, parks, farms, airports, towpaths, hospitals – yes, go into the very hospitals and wander around them. A white coat helps.

When you return, your anomie will perhaps be undiminished. Rome was not embraced in a day. You will still – unless you have been approached by a denizen of the night and accepted certain of their proposals – be alone. Yet you will have gained knowledge of your environment, will be less timorous, less apologetic, and more likely to stand up and say boldly: 'I, yes *I*, am a citizen of Slough'.

# XIII

# VIEW THE CITY FROM
# A HIGH PLACE

A truly great city, that is – Tokyo, perhaps. I recommend the view from the North Observation Deck of the Tokyo Metropolitan Building Tower near Nishi-shinjuku station. It is open until 10.30pm.

You ascend via an elevator that takes you non-stop to the 45th floor, then make your way to the observation deck. It is very sparsely peopled. A few lovers sit on the banquette seats. There is an expensive hush in the air.

Tall windows, three storeys high, give an unparalleled view of the magnificence of the city. It extends almost without visible limit, like the *ur*-forest of medieval Europe. Jewels of every imaginable water sparkle below: amethyst, ruby, beryl, chalcedony, sapphire, topaz, diamond. They flutter and dance in the great steamy hazes exhaled by the bestial activity that keeps this wasteful, magnificent place alive. Vertiginous waves rise answeringly from within you; your head reels and your knees tremble. It is your greatest desire to merge yourself with the city, to throw yourself among these baubles in careless tribute. You wish for nothing less than to evacuate yourself into the night, and if the plate glass window were not there, might well do so.

Tottering to the bar you order a drink and a packet of nuts.

# XIV

# DO A DEED OF DARKNESS

By which I mean poaching.

> Oh, good Solomon, I have been about a deed
> of darkness tonight. Oh Lord, I saw fifteen spirits
> in the forest, like white bulls; if I lie I am an arrant
> thief. Mortality haunts us: grass and hay! The
> devil's at our heels – and let's hence to the parsonage.

Lines from *The Merry Devil of Edmonton*, by an unknown hand, late 1590s. 'The deed of darkness' was deer-poaching, on the king's land, and if caught, the offender faced death.

I have scant experience of poaching but can tell you how to steal a suckling pig. Walk up to a sow and shove her roughly out of the way with a boot. Stoop to enter her ark, snaffle one of her litter and depart with it under your arm. The sow will be making noises like a clothes-iron being plunged into cold water, and the pigling will be giving forth shattering screams like brass doors being ripped from their hinges. It is therefore imperative that you do this deed at night, in a field far away from any farmer's habitation.

Farmers are strange people. Their houses smell and they have a peculiar sense of humour, and how their wives put up with them is anyone's guess.

# XV

# MEDITATE ON THE DARK AGES

The Dark Ages cover the period roughly from the end of the Roman Empire to the beginning of the medieval, a span of around 600-700 years. In this period, the Book of Kells was created; the Venerable Bede and St Cuthbert were the idols of their day ('Northumberland's Got Talent'); the rich man was in his castle, the poor man at the gate; he made them high and lowly, and ordered their estate. Ah, my vision fades.

The one thing that any historian will tell you about the Dark Ages is that they were not Dark. No, no: they were splendidly illumined by all sorts of deeds, artistic activity, histories and maps, and much sober statecraft that did not involve casual evisceration, and we know more about them, in fact, than almost any period in history except perhaps last week. Strange the way epochs and eras don't stay still in the consciousness, but are forever being re-examined, rehabilitated, demoted or discarded. It's most confusing. Just as the Dark Ages are no longer (it seems) Dark, the Enlightenment is now known to have been beset by wretched superstition and obfuscation and the Renaissance characterized by a total failure to comprehend Classical antiquity. I suppose historians would be out of a job if everything remained the way it was taught to us at school by respectable men and women, even if those self-same respectable men and women were later revealed to be alcoholics and pederasts.

If the Dark Ages were not Dark, what on earth is the use of them?

.

# XVI

# SEE A METEOR SHOWER

Nature by day is tedious. How quickly a ravishing vista ceases to be ravishing! Two minutes and we are already beginning to wonder what's for lunch, or how to get down.

At night all our senses come into play. Vision takes its rightful place as one member of the five, not master and commander of all. The fingers of a breeze stir us to the world's mystery. Night-flowering jasmine lets seep its syrupy fragrance. Take a sip of hot coffee from your thermos. Still enough, and you will hear distant horses, snorting as they dream.

Leave your cloister and journey into the velvet night, far from any inhabited place, far from men and women, their villages like glowing warts on the horizon.

It is September. Look up! The Perseids. They streak, burn turquoise and violet, live and die. It seems, on first glance, that each could bring death to millions, but in truth they are mere grains of dust, momentary particles in a bubble chamber.

If one the size of a snooker table fell on Sheffield, that city would be incinerated. However, I have no power of recommendation in these matters.

# XVII

# DINE AT THREE

In the incomparable *A Rebours* of Joris-Karl Huysmans, we read of the hero Des Esseintes: 'In winter, at five o'clock in the afternoon, when the day was drawing to a close, he breakfasted on two boiled eggs, toast and tea. At eleven o'clock he dined. During the night he drank coffee, and sometimes tea and wine, and at five o'clock in the morning, before retiring, he supped again lightly.'

That gives a rather short interval between breakfast and dinner, but I suppose it all depends on one's definition of dinner. Perhaps Huysmans was thinking of the Nottinghamshire version of dinner, which takes place at midday, followed by a lewd pudding in a gamekeeper's cottage.

I prefer to dine rather later, at around three in the morning. Sometimes alone, sometimes in company. A little company is not to be despised. A few select friends, ones who have no fear of boring you, and are thus free to be interesting.

One might choose a rather elaborate dinner. To quote Huysmans again: 'To the sound of funeral marches played by a concealed orchestra, nude negresses, wearing slippers and stockings of silver cloth with patterns of tears, served the guests.'

Then again, perhaps that line has not worn quite as well as Huysmans might have hoped. The negresses should probably be clothed and seated, and themselves served by nude white men, their penises tattooed with tiny Sowo masks, the African symbols of sisterhood.

# XVIII

# VISIT A FACTORY

How do you think sun-loungers are made? By people working at night!

(At this point I could produce statistics detailing the labour undertaken during the bombazine hours, but what would be the use? We would all know they had been garnered from the internet.)

However, to return to our *moutons*, if you stir yourself and visit a night-hive, you will not be disappointed. A Royal Mail sorting office, for example. Here is a secret. Don't imagine that a letter posted for the 3:30pm collection will reach its addressee marginally sooner than a letter posted for the 6:30pm. Quite the opposite. The 6:30 collection lies on top of the 3:30. The 3:30 must wait until the 6:30 has been dispersed. I have seen the heaps.

Or would you prefer to visit a nuclear power station? Equal amounts of low-grade nuclear waste are being dumped into the ocean at 4am as at 4pm, so all the action is there to be had. And there is nothing grander than the interior of a nuclear power station, its soaring cliffs and thoughtful pools, and always in the background the watchful, bathyspheric ponk of the Geiger counter.

Many, many toil at night.

It's to be hoped that the reader has a small private income from investments, and so is able to be there as an observer.

# IXX

# DRIVE AT NIGHT

Many people dislike night-driving. This is quite natural: at night the visual sense is attenuated. People fear they will lose control and crash, and suffer injury or death. They shun the embarrassment of the casualty ward. Will they have to wait in a corridor forever, bloodied and in pain, while pretty nurses ignore them?

These fears are misplaced. Nurses are no more alluring than any other segment of the general population. Nor are you more likely to have an accident at night.

And think what you may be missing!

Mayfair at four in the morning, the Savile Club illuminated and yet deserted within, bath chairs empty and clocks tocking their way toward the morning delivery of *The Times*. Dark country hills where headlights start eyes from the hedgerows. A lit motorway like a necklace of rare amber. A phone mast tipped with the merest drop of scintillating blood.

If you do drive over a roe deer, that is not necessarily to be regretted. Make sure it is properly dead, and then carefully incise around its anus. Remove the internal organs, skin and head, then joint it for the freezer. Do not attempt to keep any part as a trophy: it will attract flies.

# READ A BOOK

What to read at three in the morning? A comedy? Surely not. Nothing stirs outside your shutters. Obtenebration reigns. Dreams and nightmares have taken the place of television programmes in the minds of the sleeping nation. (Though perhaps the nation is dreaming of those self-same television programmes, and is appearing unaccountably naked in *The Only Way is Essex*.) This is the time for something serious, strange, weighty.

What to choose? Allow me to suggest *In Praise of Shadows* (1933) by Junichiro Tanizaki, a book that deals with nuances of dimness and duskiness that could only be savoured in an era before electric illumination. In one of its most celebrated passages, the author meditates at some length on the ideal spot for an outside toilet:

> The Japanese toilet truly is a place of spiritual repose. It always stands apart from the main building, at the end of a corridor, in a grove fragrant with leaves and moss. No words can describe that sensation as one sits in the dim light, basking in the faint glow reflected from the *shoji*, lost in meditation or gazing out at the garden. The novelist Natsume Soseki counted his trips to the toilet a great pleasure, a 'physiological delight' as he called it. [...] And the toilet is the perfect place to listen to the chirping of insects or the song of the birds, to view the moon, or to enjoy any of those poignant moments that mark the change of the seasons. Here, I suspect, is where haiku poets over the ages have come by a great many of their ideas.

# JOIN A PARTY UNINVITED

This is very easy to do. By two o'clock in the morning even the most punctilious host has ceased to care.

Simply ring at the door and say: 'I live nearby and heard the noise. Rather than lying in bed for the next three hours with my head pressed into the pillow, gnashing my teeth and wishing death and destruction on you all, I have decided to offer whatever contribution I can to the general merriment.'

If ringing at the door elicits no response, don't give up. Investigate the basement, where there may be an unlocked window. Make your way to the upper floors. Following the noise, throw open the door, revealing three schoolboys sitting around a bottle of cider. All right, you have made a mistake.

It is surprising what can follow from attending a party uninvited. You might make new friends. You might find something to eat and drink. You might be able to have a bath.

Soaking in strange bathrooms at night, frothing up a stranger's bubble bath with one listless hand while music thuds from below, is very enjoyable. If anyone wishes to come in to use the lavatory, let them. It is not your place to enforce petty prohibitions.

# XXII

# MEDITATE

Many years ago, when I first studied Transcendental Meditation, I was instructed to take a piece of fruit wrapped in a clean handkerchief to my guru. The request struck me as interesting: one the one hand, who would want a piece of fruit in a dirty handkerchief? Wasn't the injunction that it should be clean somewhat superfluous? Did the guru have a low opinion of the personal habits of his neophytes? On the other, after scoffing the fruit, what did he do with all the handkerchiefs? He then gave me my personalized mantra and told me never to divulge it to anyone (it is 'Engar-ay'). Following that, I had my first practice meditation session in a cramped living room with ten other recruits, many of whom, having come straight from work, were struggling to stay awake.

I was also told by the fat and rather unclean little guru not to meditate at night, since meditation was intended to refresh and awaken the mind for one's day-time activities. This advice was punctuated by the snores of several of those present.

I have often ignored his advice completely, as I desire to have a refreshed and awakened mind at around 2am.

# XXIII

# LISTEN TO INSECTS

One of the delights of the tropics is the sound of insects at night: somehow these tiny creatures have great power to comfort the lonely and wakeful. Never mind that they are rubbing themselves in a sort of masturbatory delirium. That is their business.

In the tropics it is also possible to listen to kittens mewing in a drain. I experienced this while in Singapore. Uncharacteristically, I was trying to get to sleep at 3am, possibly due to the effects of jetlag, when I was disturbed by a plaintive wailing. Going out into the humid night, I found a pair of kittens abandoned in a storm drain behind the house. I rolled my sleeves up and proceeded to extricate them, wishing I had worn gloves (they scratched). I then took them back into the house and put them into a cardboard box with some milk. The next day I rang around the various local authorities to see if I could find them a home. I was met with irritation. No one wanted them. My twin foundlings were surplus to the island's limited feline requirements. I finally paid a humanitarian agency to take them away, and, with a cowardice of which I am still ashamed, did not ask what their fate would be. The following night I heard the same pathetic cries emanating from another storm drain just a little way off from the first. I covered my ears.

# XXIV

# SEE FIREFLIES

'The glow worm shows the matin to be near / And 'gins to pale his uneffectual fire,' as we learn from *Hamlet*. The glow-worm, here, is the firefly. There's no difference. They are both names for insects of the family *Lampyridae*, which create a faint illumination in their nether parts via the enzyme luciferase. Lucifer – the bringer of light. Also, formerly, a match. 'While you've a Lucifer to light your fag, then smile, boys, smile.'

'And 'gins to pale his uneffectual fire.' *Pale fire*. Ah, so Nabokov was quoting Shakespeare. The firefly is replete with literary associations.

Where to see a firefly? Try somewhere far from anywhere you yet know, and then further. Go to a bog, a marsh, a wood, a wild place where no turpitude of man can interfere with the 'uneffectuality' of the firefly's efforts. Like a dowser, make for water and damp and trickling sounds. Fireflies are found on every continent except Antarctica, so unless you are exceptionally unlucky and are reading this on a scientific base surrounded by sexually frustrated Norwegians with a five-month growth of beard, fireflies will be somewhere within a few hundred miles of your present location.

Take proper clothing, of course. Wellington boots, several pairs of trousers, an astrakhan coat. A folding chair. Now wait. You may be lucky.

# SEE THE IGNIS FATUUS

The *ignis fatuus*, or will o' the wisp, is a bluish light that seems to emanate from marshy or swampy ground, only to recede if you try to get near it. Milton knew of it:

Compact of unctuous vapour, which the night
Condenses, and the cold environs round
Kindled through agitation to a flame...

Its name means 'foolish fire', perhaps because those who have seen it are not believed, or perhaps because those who try to approach it are lured to a reedy, muddy death. Not so much foolish as fatal, perhaps.

What is the *ignis fatuus*? One guess is that it is produced by methane emanating from swampy land, which is then ignited by lightning. Other theories involve the bioluminescence of honey fungus and the discharge of geo-electricity under tectonic strain (though none of these theories explains why it appears to recede when approached). Barn owls have also been fingered. So I hear.

# TAKE THE NIGHT TRAIN

'This is the night mail, crossing the Border / bringing the cheque and the postal order.' Many readers will remember the poem. It accompanied a film called 'Night Mail', made in the 1930s, which followed the journey of the Royal Mail express from London to Glasgow, carrying the 'letters from banks, letters of thanks' etc. vital to the nation. The words were written by WH Auden. Others may have 'Stop all the clocks' read at their funeral, but I would like 'Night Mail.' It will be worth it for the frowns of perplexity on the faces of the few that have convened for my sending-off:

> Pulling up Beattock, a steady climb:
> The gradient's against her, but she's on time.

Indeed. On time. Well, everyone is on time for their own funeral. It is the one event where you simply have to be there. And all will become clear by the end of the poem. For the last lovely lines are:

> And none will hear the postman's knock
> Without a quickening of the heart,
> For who can bear to feel himself forgotten?

Yes, Uncle Alex was a subtle one, my niblings will whisper one to another.

# XXVII

# TAKE AN ACTUAL
# NIGHT TRAIN

The foregoing is strictly the night mail, rather than the night train, and unless you are a postal worker or Buster Edwards, you cannot 'take the Night Mail'. But you can take a night train. There is enormous romance in a sleeper.

I am reminded of a passage in a Chekhov short story in which a group of soldiers are telling tall tales around a camp-fire. One says that he was once in a pitch-dark sleeper in which the only other occupant was an unknown young lady. Suddenly the train jolts and the young lady is thrown against him, 'breasts like buffers, nostrils breathing fire, lips the colour of the best salmon.' One of the other soldiers interrupts: 'I agree that such a thing might have happened,' he says, 'but how could you see what colour her lips were if it was dark?'

If you want a truly authentic night train experience, consider something such as the overnight express from Nairobi to Mombasa, where the experience has not been ruined by consciousness of itself as an 'experience', as in the 'Orient Express Experience' or some such nonsense. Naturally you should avoid going too far in the other direction so that the train has no seats and there is running human waste in the aisles.

# XXVIII

# BROOD ON THE PAST –
# AND THE FUTURE

There is no past, in any real sense: it is only memory, a phenomenon of the mind. Even less is there a future: it has not happened yet. So the only way to fully comprehend and enjoy life is to live in the present.

But what anti-human philosophy!

Of course we live in the past. Of course we roll it around our mouths and savour it in the gathering dark. Naturally we brood on it, caress it, cherish it, hold it close. We are our memories, our opinions, the wisdom we have gleaned. Take away our pasts and we are condemned to a monotonous incarceration in the present moment, a moment in which the only thing in the world is the evidence of our brute senses. 'How is your egg?' This is why people jump out of planes. Well, thrills have their place. But one may experience thrills by lying in the dark and remembering.

Of course we live in the future. Of course we build castles in Spain, carry the very mortar in our hods. What incomparable excitement to *make a plan*! What a unique human endeavour: to see the glowing and pulsing ball of the possible take shape in our fancy! What do you, dear reader, hope for? Much, I imagine. But you cannot hope for something that is already right there under your nose.

Live in the present? An activity for cows!

# MAKE CANDLES OF ICE

For this one needs very cold weather, though it can also be done with a freezer. Simply take a large cylindrical container with smooth sides, such as a bucket, and fill it with water. Set it outside to freeze. Leave it there until a thickish crust of ice has formed on the top, then remove it into the warm and let it defrost for about half an hour. (To accelerate the process, place it in a bath of warm water.) Now decant the ice candle from the cylinder. You will notice that the candle is hollow: the freezing process has started at the top and sides of the container, but the interior is still liquid. Usually the base is also unfrozen. You are in possession of a hollow ice cylinder.

Set your ice candle upside down and remove any ice from the top (formerly the base). Your ice candle now has a frozen bottom and sides. Put a tea light in the bottom, and set it outside to welcome travellers. Or place it in your rooms and watch as the beams of the tea candle, fractured by the ice, cast strange lights over your walls.

# XXX

# PLAY PATIENCE

There are numerous types of patience, though I play only one. I get it out about once in every twenty goes – a satisfying rate of failure.

Death's-head patience is the version played in the short story 'The Seventh Pullet' by Saki. A mild-mannered commuter passes the time by telling lies to his train companions. His first lie concerns an incident in which his chickens are attacked by a snake: the snake hypnotizes and kills six of the chickens, but fails to kill the seventh because it has a crest of feathers hanging over its eyes and can't see the snake. The chicken then pecks the snake to death. The story makes the man an instant celebrity, which he finds intoxicating, and he invent further stories to satisfy his listeners. After his third or fourth lie, his friends begin to suspect him.

Finally, something really astonishing does happen to him: one evening he notices his wife playing a game she calls 'Death's-head patience'. 'I've never got it out,' she tells him, 'and I'm almost there. My mother and grand-aunt only got it out once, and they both died immediately afterwards, thus the name.' 'Well, you can do it if you put that five of clubs there on the open six,' says the man. 'Oh yes,' says the wife, then keels over on the spot. The next day the man goes into work and tells the story to his friends, but they just laugh at him. It is the only astonishing thing that has ever happened to him, and they don't believe him.

I've rather ruined it for you now.

# XXXI

# INVENT A NEW
# BOARD GAME

You can do this quite easily. Take a piece of cardboard and draw a circuit or pathway of some kind on it. Now divide the circuit or pathway into squares and assign values of some kind to each square. You could create a board game called 'Pilgrim's Progress', for example, in which the squares represent 'the Slough of Despond', 'the Castle of Doubt', and so on. One of my games, 'Duodenum', has a route like an intestine. Assign consequences to various squares, such as 'Go back five spaces', 'Pay a forfeit', etc. You can also create props such as question cards and multi-sided dice, but these are rather fiddly.

In one of my games, 'British Slime Moulds', the idea is to play with reference books found around the home: a dictionary, a cookbook, an atlas, and British Slime Moulds. Each square refers you to one of the books. In the case of the dictionary square, you name a random page, column and number, and your neighbour looks up the word at that location, tells you what it is and asks you to define it. In the case of the cookbook, your neighbour gives you a recipe (e.g. 'brown trout with almonds'), and you must name three ingredients mentioned in the recipe that are not in the title (you get five tries and cannot name salt, pepper, or oil). In the case of the atlas, your neighbour names a country, and you must name two countries bordering it (in four tries).

In the case of British Slime Moulds, you must identify the slime mould.

# XXXII

# LISTEN TO THE WORLD SERVICE

The World Service, I learned to my disappointment in childhood, is broadcast in English. Broadcasting does apparently take place in other languages, but one cannot tune in and hear Albanian, Farsi and Xhosa from a bedroom in the Home Counties. Not on my radio, at least. Still, it passes an idle hour at 2am.

As all bores know, the best thing on the radio at night is the Shipping Forecast, though this is actually broadcast on Radio 4 just before and after the World Service begins and ends, since Chadian tribesmen, while they might be interested in the news in order to keep tabs on the iniquities of their own government, are unlikely to be concerned as to wind strength and direction in North Utsire.

At times when listening to the World Service, I have the strong sense that I am the only person left alive in the world, and thus that all the taxpayers' money that has been pumped into the Service is exclusively for my benefit.

Or I might tune in between channels, so there is nothing but a hiss, with faint irruptions of chatter in unidentifiable tongues, the babble of lives led elsewhere, people so far-flung they might be the denizens of other stars.

# XXXIII

# WONDER WHETHER
# THE NAZIS COULD HAVE
# WON THE WAR

The night is a time for speculation on the *what ifs* of history.
What if the D-Day landings had failed? What if Winston
Churchill had been three foot tall with terrible eczema? I
suppose, in an infinite universe, anything that *can* happen
*will* happen. The question is not so much whether the Nazis
could have won the war, but how to stop them coming to get
us from any of the infinite number of parallel universes in
which they did.

I am not an historian; I am not indeed 'an' anything.
But it seems obvious to me that Hitler's attempt to conquer
Russia was the act of a suicidal madman. And yet if you
raise the matter with an historian he will tell you: 'It was
vital in 1941 that Hitler strike east: he was running out of
oil.' He might as well say 'He was running out of cheese': I
cannot comment. I have not seen the documents. I do not
speak German or Russian. But can the historian speak German or Russian? Ha! Address a few words to him in either
of those languages. What? Is he forming his opinion from
second-hand sources? Outrageous! Then I say, and say most
firmly: there was a terminal Camembert shortage in the Europe of 1941, the Nazis having obliterated the French cheese
industry by incompetent bombing. Only the stocks of Brie
and Rocquefort known to have been accumulated by Stalin
in secret bunkers in the Kremlin could appease Hitler's lac-
tophiliac Wehrmacht. Thus the fatal die was cast.

# XXXIV

# SHARE THE NIGHT WITH
# AN OHAGURO GIRL

This is no longer possible, so it is not in reality a 'thing to do'. It can be accomplished in the imagination only.

*Ohaguro* was the Japanese practice, now long dead, of blackening the teeth. Women would deliberately darken their teeth with ash or lacquer in order to make themselves more beautiful. To appreciate this requires some mental adjustment in the present epoch, where spotless snowy enamel is the goal of all.

After dyeing her teeth black, the *ohaguro* girl would shave off her eyebrows, powder her face a deathly white, and then, in Kyoto style, paint her lips green. With the last trace of blood-pink removed from her face, and raven locks framing the whole, the ideal of Japanese womanly perfection would be achieved: an eerie Noh mask. Imagine that thing looming from a candle-lit interior, glints of gold and strange fish and cranes swirling on her kimono, and then, leaning toward you, something like a skinned victim, a monster with its face torn off, and where the mouth should be, a gaping toothless hole, a gaping hole ready to swallow you up, breathing greenly at you from the darkness and offering you a bowl of tea?

# HAVE AN ASSIGNATION
# IN A DARKENED ROOM

Of course you can't just ring up and order an assignation in a darkened room. These things take planning.

One method might be to muscle in on someone else's assignation in a darkened room. It's dark, so they won't know who you are. You will be able to steal at least one kiss before a shriek of horror wakes the slumbering house!

Actually I confess that this idea is taken from a short story previously alluded to – 'The Kiss', by Anton Pavlovich Chekhov. The plot relies crucially on darkness. A sad, undistinguished little gunner called Ryabovsky (or is it Ryachevsky – or neither?) is attending a party at a country house. He wanders around, watches some fellow officers playing billiards, and then stumbles by mistake into a dark room, where a young woman, mistaking him for her lover, plants a kiss on his lips before realising her error and running off. The soldier too rushes out into the light, convinced that everyone will know what has just happened and that there will be uproar: but the party goes on as before. Slowly a feeling of joy takes hold of him, and he begins to think that he too is destined for happiness. He looks around him at all the young women present and tries to guess which one it must have been ('Take the shoulders from that one, and the eyes from that one...') And this time you'll have to read the story to discover the end. Please believe me when I say it is one of the masterworks of 19th-century European literature.

# XXXVI

# CONTEMPLATE
# THE ISLE OF THE DEAD

I used to know the name of the painter of this work; it has slipped my mind. Arnold Böcklin, perhaps. Suffice it to say that this painting is the consummate depiction of Night. It depicts a gloom-enshrouded islet, with in its centre a stand of cypresses. The outer edges of the islet are dominated by sandstone cliffs in which strange doors, perhaps the openings to tombs, are carved. Approaching in a little boat are two figures, one rowing and the other, garbed in white, standing at the prow. In front of the standing figure is a draped coffin, no doubt shortly to be interned in one of the rock-cut mausolea. It is so dark that the sky and the sea, which is of a millpond stillness, are the same murky viridian hue, and yet the island itself, and especially the white-garbed figure, are lit up with an otherworldly luminosity. It is that effect of light that gives the picture its magic? For the island and its crags are gold with the burnish of an Antique temple. And who is that robed figure in the prow, standing supernaturally erect? If the water is the Styx and the ferryman is Charon, is this Jesus Christ in the world of the Greek Dead?

No wonder this canvas was so popular in 19th-century parlours: respectable middle-class Victorians could fantasize that Christ, in some symbolic act, was bringing together the Classical world and the modern; and every Christian Miss, her mind inflamed by tales of Artemis and Actaeon, of Orpheus and Eurydice, could pant after a pagan death.

The Isle of the Dead gives each of us a chance to fill that coffin with someone we have loved, or with ourselves.

# LISTEN TO VIVALDI'S
# LA NOTTE

This is the most beautiful piece of music ever composed on the theme of Night.

Vivaldi composed several concerti for flute and strings; this is one of them. It has six movements: slow, quick, slow, quick, slow and quick. (They may be *adagios*, *largos*, *allegros* or *prestos*.) The fifth movement is one of the most syrupy pieces in all of the baroque repertoire. It can't be more than twenty notes long, yet it is drawn out with astonishing loveliness. And the final fast movement that follows is one of the sprightliest pieces in the oeuvre of this sprightliest of all composers. It is like flying over a village on Christmas Eve, seeing the twinkling lights of cottages, revelling in the boisterous clouds and wind.

I do not recommend listening to *La Notte* while contemplating *The Isle of the Dead*: that painting merits instead something by Wagner, featuring horned helmets and breast-plated storm-maidens. Vivaldi is an artist of life, not death; love, not war. Perhaps instead a dusk-scene by one of the great humanists of painting, such as Vivaldi's contemporary Claude Lorrain: one of his great landscape fantasias, featuring mysterious castles melting in submarine greens and blues and silvers.

XXXVIII

# DON'T LEARN A LANGUAGE

If you can't sleep, then learning a language will send you to sleep.

Really, there is no need for an English-speaker to learn another language. You often hear people saying that in ten years' time everyone will be speaking Mandarin – an opinion formed through the excessive turning upside-down of small manufactured products and seeing what is written there – but this is quite untrue. The Chinese are hard at work learning English. There are eight times as many people actively learning English in China as actually live in England. Learning Mandarin will only annoy them. They have, after all, spent years of their lives and a considerable fraction of their incomes learning to say 'excuse me, my daughter has a throat infection'. Not learning Mandarin is an act of common courtesy – not to say Confucian wisdom – on our part.

It pains me to say this, but in the very near future instantaneous communication via electronic translation devices will be available to all, and when you wish to say 'Excuse me, I think you dropped this egg' to a beautiful Xunganese boy, you will simply select the Xunganese option from a menu on your handheld device, speak into it in English, and it will deliver your message in fluent and idiomatic Xunganese to the recipient.

不必要

# XXXIX

# VISIT A CHURCH

You may find a church that isn't locked, especially in an out-of-the-way country place. Or go on a winter's evening, before closing time. Visiting a church is among the greatest of all night-time recreations. We speak of night life: there is also night death. Sit amid the aching stones in the sepulchral silence, under the bloody body and glazed eyes of a brutalised and crucified god, and you will see what I mean. 'A serious house on serious earth it is', as Philip Larkin, Yoda-like, put it.

The Bible does night very well. The Garden of Gethsemane and its night-agony. The nativity, its supernova-illuminated angels, shepherds and kings. Jonah in the blackness of the whale's belly, Jacob dream-wrestling with the angel, ascending heavenward on a ladder of fire. The night of the Last Supper, Jesus and his disciples, thirteen at table. 'He who made the Pleiades and Orion...who calls for the waters of the sea and pours them out on the surface of the earth...'

Lord, do not crucify me as you crucified your son. Grant my fragile body and fluttering mind respite from torment. I do not wish to pass through the furnace, even if I emerge as gold. I am satisfied with tin. Protect me. Take the cup of suffering from me.

And will my cries be, in Hopkins's words, 'like dead letters sent / To dearest him that lives alas! away'?

# XL

# READ 'I WAKE AND FEEL THE FELL OF DARK, NOT DAY' BY GERALD MANLEY HOPKINS

... from which sonnet the quote at the end of the last section is taken. Hopkins wakes at night, hoping for light, then realises that there is a long struggle yet to endure till dayfall. It is the same struggle he has endured throughout all the years of his young Jesuit life: battling doubt and temptation of the flesh, conscious of sin with a consciousness as sharp as his consciousness of beauty. He yearns for a treasure eyesight never got, and looks to God, recking His rod. He burns in the shame of being himself.

I wake and feel the fell of dark, not day.
What hours, O what black hoürs we have spent
This night! what sights you, heart, saw; ways you went!
And more must, in yet longer light's delay.
With witness I speak this. But where I say
Hours I mean years, mean life. And my lament
Is cries countless, cries like dead letters sent
To dearest him that lives alas! away.

I am gall, I am heartburn. God's most deep decree
Bitter would have me taste: my taste was me;
Bones built in me, flesh filled, blood brimmed the curse.
Selfyeast of spirit a dull dough sours. I see
The lost are like this, and their scourge to be
As I am mine, their sweating selves; but worse.

58

# XLI

# TRESPASS IN THE GARDENS OF EX-LOVERS

Here, perhaps, you had a moonlight tryst; there you sat and picnicked; there, under that soaring pear tree, you strolled and chatted. All past now, along with those hot kisses, those languorous sighs, those desperate fumblings. She (or he) has 'moved on'. A new lover lights up eyes and loins. You, however, have not 'moved on'. You have defied the policeman of the heart, and continue to loiter. You remain at the scene of this crime, even though, strictly speaking, it is private property.

What is your lover doing now? And more importantly, with whom? It is one o'clock in the morning. The hour of love. You lean on the birdbath, alert to any noise from the upstairs bedroom windows. The night is sultry. Was that a gasp, a sigh, a cry? You go closer to the house and press your ear against the glass of the conservatory. Is that a vibration of springs? Is the deep breathing your own? Do all slumber within?

Or perhaps you come earlier, at eleven. Through the kitchen window, you see them there together. She retrieves a cookbook from a shelf and looks at it pensively. He walks up behind her and sadly puts his arms around her waist. They stand, for a long time. They are unhappy together. Your lover has exchanged you for unhappiness, and what's more, gained on the deal.

No need to paint your face with mud; you have become invisible.

# XLII

# DRINK

I begin around nine. I ease myself into my night of debauch with a simple gin and tonic. I have some music playing: something energizing, like a Brandenburg Concerto. I toss off some postcards.

Next, a pint of traditional cider, tasting of wasps and mud. I keep active, doing the washing up or singing. Now it's time to start on the wine. A nice Blue Nun that I've been keeping locked up in the basement since the 1970s: I make her last until around eleven. I do not slump into an armchair in front of the television, or, even more fatally, start eating.

Now, as midnight shakes the memory, some ales. A keg is useful at this stage, and holding one's head underneath the spigot is good exercise. I alternate with mulled perry. Spices to taste: cinnamon, cloves, mace, nutmeg, Bisto. I pull on rubber gloves and begin shouting.

Two o'clock. I experiment with meat cocktails: beef screwdriver, lamb and a splash, mutton wallbanger. There has in fact been banging on the walls for some time. I go into the street wearing only my '#1 Dad' barbecue apron given by an ironic ex-lover and solicit passing men. One glass of port (no more). A lonely chime of three.

More ale, this time bottle-conditioned: I recommend Ill-Tempered Gnome, Collapsed-Bridge Troll, Restraining-Order Elf. Four. Dawn is gilding the rooves. I throw aside even my apron and wander the public gardens clutching a half-bottle of Tokay. Every blade of grass drips dew-universes. I lie in their sweetness, dreaming of a Polish girl called Rosa.

## XLIII

# STROLL IN THE DAY OF YOUR IMAGINATION

Night has many charms, but certain activities are proscribed. One cannot ring up a builder to have ones gutters cleared, or go to the library, or the fish market, or an Italian restaurant. They are all closed. Of course, the fact that they are closed has its own appeal. At 4am one can gaze in at the window of an Italian restaurant and reflect that Italian culture and cuisine is ultimately doomed, and that when the reckoning finally comes for all things Italian, all Italian restaurants will be as this one, silent, forlorn, abandoned, no longer filled with strutting oiled dandiprats and offering as sustenance nothing but the disappointment of pasta.

Yet one cannot deny that night excludes certain possibilities. Why not enjoy them instead in your imagination?

Focus on something in your room. A roll of masking tape. Now remember where you bought it – perhaps in the hardware shop. Remember the mixed scents of raw wood, emulsion and nails (nails have a smell). There was a woman peering like a heron at some hose attachments. In the background the shuffling of sweaty training shoes. In your mouth, the taste of the pork and apple sauce roll you inadvisably bought in the market. Make your way out of the hardware shop and back to that roll vendor to complain about it, annihilating him. Stroll around the town, calling in at the shops, seeing the haircuts, overhearing conversations, feeling the sun's rays, smelling the odours of dust, traffic and money.

# XLIV

# GO INTO THE FOREST AND
# BURN YOUR POEMS

This is one of my favourite night-time recreations, and I hope readers will take it up with equal enthusiasm. Simply gather up all your verse meditations on love and death, take them to a secluded spot in the forest, douse them with lighter fluid and immolate them. This results in a wonderful feeling of liberation and a renewed desire to create afresh. Just think: the next poem you write will be the very first of your future oeuvre to survive into posterity. (At least it will be if you don't then burn every subsequent poetic accumulation, as I strongly recommend you do.)

If there is no forest nearby, try a golf course. Place the poems in the centre of one of its expensively-manicured greens and set them ablaze. There are few more prosaic venues than a golf course – the haunt by day of solicitors and car salesmen – and burning poetry is very much in the spirit of the place. Indeed, one gets the feeling that many among the golfing fraternity would like to burn poets as well as poems.

You will leave an ugly black mark and a melted flag that will need replacing, but perhaps club members will see this as a reasonable price to pay for the destruction of some of the nation's verse.

# XLV

# GO FOR A WALK

A walk in the day is all fine and good, but a walk in the night... where every object is silvered with mystery, and no one is there to interfere...

That house has a fine flight of steps. Why not stride up them and stand, one hand on the head of that pocked stone lion, pretending you are the householder?

On Sunday at 4.30 am, make the rounds of the postboxes, crammed full for Monday: put your hands in the slits and feel the letters, like a child on Christmas Eve feeling his pillowcase.

Find a cricket pavilion and try the door: it is unlocked. Go inside and switch on the tea-urn. See if there are any biscuits.

(Eschew all works of the day. Even to sleep is a work of the day, because it makes the day possible.)

Saturated with beauty, light a cigarette and give yourself an infinitesimally greater chance of a hideous death. The bell tolls the hour.

Go to the edge of a pond. Geese will sail silently up to you in the gloom. Little do they know that you have burned all your poems and have nothing for them.

# XLVI

# TELL A STORY AROUND
# A CAMPFIRE

If you find yourself around a roaring log fire at night on the beach or in the woods, you may be challenged to produce a story. I recommend you tell this one.

'Many years ago, when I was still happily married, and before the great disaster that brought me here to this lonely spot, my family and I used to spend our evenings quietly reading and talking in the parlour. One night, we heard a noise coming from behind the chimney breast. It was a fluttering, scraping sound: obviously a bird had flown down the chimney and become trapped. Perhaps it was wounded. The children pleaded with me to do something about it, but I could see that this would be difficult: a gas fire lay in front of the old hearth, and the only way to rescue the bird would be to dismantle the fire. Now, I have no experience in fitting or unfitting gas fires, and am not particularly good with my hands. My wife urgently requested that I desist pulling at the pipes that held the thing to the wall, but the children's cries drove me on, and with what now seems to me recklessness I ripped the thing from its moorings, rupturing a pipe and causing a shrill of gas to discharge itself into the room. Unfortunately a single Advent candle was burning on the mantelpiece, which ignited the gas, causing a terrific explosion which killed everyone present.'

You should then stand up and walk off, fading into the surrounding night.

# WRITE DOWN YOUR DREAMS

If we did not do it, could we imagine that something so bizarre as dreaming could possibly occur? That is, that as soon as we drifted into unconsciousness, forces unreachable during our waking hours would take command of our thoughts, like a clown elbowing aside a dead pilot, and that we would become, not the thinkers of our thoughts, but their observers? And that the dream-worlds weaving themselves in our skulls would be so vivid that on awaking we would be unsure as to what was dream and what real, and, in the poet's words, would 'cry to dream again'?

'Other people's dreams are about as interesting as other people's children.' Correct, but that need not inhibit us from recording our dreams. They will always be fascinating to their progenitors, if no one else. And there may be nuggets of dreamgold that are truly useful. In the 1880s a chemist called Kekule went to bed worrying about the molecular structure of benzene, and dreamed of a snake with its tail in its mouth. When he woke he realised that benzene takes the form of a ring. 'Well, naturally,' we might say now.

If you get into a similar habit you may find on waking that you have invented a machine for extracting gold from cat excrement.

Dreams are invaluable to the fiction-writer. They must have inspired Kafka's famous *Metamorphosis*. After all, if you dream that you are a beetle, how can you be sure that on waking you are not a beetle dreaming that it is you?

# WRITE DOWN YOUR NIGHTMARES

Simone de Beauvoir had a recurring nightmare. She dreamed that she went to bed at twenty and woke up an old woman of fifty, all her youth and beauty gone. When she did finally wake she found she was twenty again, with her life still before her, and experienced such relief that she almost wept. However, this was still part of the dream. On actually waking, she found she was fifty. Imagine the final and irrevocable horror of that.

I once dreamed of reading the newspaper when a large black housefly landed on it and established itself on the face of Prince Edward. I shook the paper, but it just sat there, rubbing its forelegs together. I felt a strong repulsion for the insect, its filthy hairiness and its quick limbs and pulpy eyes, and shook the paper again, but it refused to move. I stood and brandished the paper violently in the direction of a wastepaper basket, hoping to funnel the fly down and into this receptacle. I succeeded, and went off to sit in another chair some way away, just in case the fly wished to crawl out of the basket and establish itself once more on the face of the seventh in line to the throne. I took up my newspaper. To my horror I saw that the fly was on the back of my hand! Filthy and black and massive! The fly, the fly, the hideous fly!

Well, I thought it was effective.

# WRITE A LETTER TO YOUR FUTURE SELF

Dear future self,

You are older and uglier than I am now. That is a fact. However, you may be having much more fun that I am. A strange paradox. You are crippled and sagging, be-jowled and ashy of head, but you are having a riotous time all the same. The happiest age is 73, I have heard it said. Is that much-promised thing, wisdom, responsible? Surely not in your case. You repel wisdom as tripe repels teenage girls. You make as many ill-advised remarks, are as crassly insensitive, and are subject to the same tempestuous moods as you were when you were thirty-five, or six. Perhaps you have grown into your foolishness, as Lear did: 'I am a foolish fond old man.' Perhaps you have found someone to be fond with. It is undeniable that in the past you have been terribly alone. Perhaps your companion is also sagging and mouldy, with a face like wet washing fallen from a line, but nevertheless delights you with their wit, and knows what youth meant in the 1950s (or 40s, 60s, 80s). At any rate, I salute you, and from my slightly less lined and hideous present offer you the hand of fellowship. You and I have much in common. We are the same person.

Yours etc.
Present self.

# L

# WRITE A LETTER TO YOUR PAST SELF

Dear past self,

There is great satisfaction in writing to one's past self: one knows so much that is useful for one's past self to know. For example, it was a bad idea to spend so long choosing a gift at Ankara airport, because one missed one's connecting flight. However, there is also great frustration: it is impossible to relay that information to one's past self because the universe is organized in a vexingly linear fashion. Nevertheless, I write to you in the hope that you can somehow hear me through filaments of time more erratic than those usually experienced.

Now, in these circumstances, one is prone to act the Dutch uncle. 'In 1983, don't cross that railway line on foot.' 'In 1992, do answer the policeman courteously.' But I won't offer any advice: you are entitled to your own mistakes, and the resilience of youth will enable you to endure the consequences (amputation; incarceration). Instead, I have questions. What does it feel like to have hair? What inner fire leads you to think that Tolstoy is more important than copulation? Why, exactly, is a mortgage, a system of having a roof and bed available to one when one needs it, to be so frankly despised? What is it like to be so unafraid, nihilistic, contemptuous, crazed, sane and miserable? Please write the answers in a letter (see the previous section).

Yours etc.
Future self.

# PLAY NIGHT TENNIS

Playing tennis in the dark is not an uncommon activity. That's what floodlights are for, after all. However, it's possible to play with no illumination whatever.

What? I hear you cry. Tennis for the blind? In which the players locate each other, bat-like, through their cries alone? No, not at all. In night tennis the court is marked out with fluorescent lines, the ball is a day-glo pink, the players wear fluorescent jackets and wield fluorescent rackets. The net glows softly. Once you get your eye in, you find that it makes just as much sense as day tennis, if not more.

There are a few differences. For example, the strawberries and cream traditional at diurnal tennis matches are replaced by carrots and cream, since they tend to promote good vision. Minor royals are asked to wear luminescent tiaras. Ugly tennis players garner as many worshippers as beautiful ones.

In fact, other sports should be played in darkness. Night javelin, for example, would be interesting; or night hammer-throw. I would give a considerable amount never to see another footballer. And it would be amusing to find the sports pages entirely filled with black squares.

# LII

# SEE THE DAWN

Dawn occurs remarkably early in summer. In the British Isles, the earliest is around half past four, though the welkin is beginning to bleach well before that, perhaps as early as three. This is not night, in that it is not dark, but it might as well be. There are no people in the streets or cars in the roads: one can lie down on the asphalt, roll around and lick it, if one has a mind.

What is it about the dawn that has inspired poets? Difficult to say. Perhaps it is that poets usually get up around 11, and thus, for them, dawn is an impossibly glamorous time of day. Who was it said of Samuel Johnson that the only place he was likely to have greeted the rosy-fingered dawn was in a verse of Homer?

The dawn, of course, heralds day, a time of retreat and rest after the exertions of night. The birds know this: they quieten down considerably soon after the sun rises, having exhausted themselves twittering for the past hour about their sexual prowess and the extent of their real estate. As soon as the sun, that improbable ball of exploding hydrogen, looms above the fence of the world, the syrupy gurgle of the blackbird, the fluting warble of the robin, the braying of the wren are heard no more.

# SEE THE AURORA AUSTRALIS

One can see the *aurora borealis*, or northern lights, from Canada, Greenland, Russia, Finland, Iceland and other northerly territories. People go to these places with their children; and if the northern lights don't put in an appearance, cheer themselves with hearty activities offered by their blonde be-pigtailed hosts: ice-bowling, snow-tubing, tour-skating, igloo building, husky-sledding, snowmobiling. The northern lights are very democratic, not to say demotic. You can see them any time from April to September. You can see them on a boat or with a goat, as Dr Seuss might have put it.

In contrast, very few people alive have ever seen the *aurora australis*, or southern lights.

The reason is that down there, in the south, there is no land to see them from – apart from Antarctica. And very few people have been to Antarctica. To get there you need to take a boat over thousands of miles of berg-choked sea, and once there, face life in a cruel and barren environment with no trees, cities, running water or blonde instructors. If you run out of bully beef, you may have to eat your own dogs, though you should not eat their livers: the surfeit of Vitamin A will cause all the skin from your lower limbs and genitals to fall off.

Much in life is not about what one does, but how one does it. The *aurora australis* is essentially identical in appearance to the *aurora borealis*, but if one sees it with flayed genitals and gnawing on seal blubber, suffering from scurvy, dehydration and hypothermia, the experience is likely to be that much more memorable.

LIV

# DETERMINE WHETHER THE DARKEST HOUR REALLY IS JUST BEFORE DAWN

Frankly, I will leave you to conduct this experiment. I know the answer. Hint: is the lightest hour just before the dusk?

Of course the saying has a metaphorical application, and this has rather blinded people as to its actual veracity. In any case, no one wishes to get up early enough to check. It is comforting to believe that at the point of greatest emotional agony or intellectual obnubilation, relief is at hand; and a memorable phrase is needed to encapsulate this belief.

(It is strange how important the untrue is to all aspects of human life. We wish to believe that our movements have meaning, that events have significance. Our worldviews are salted with canards. You catch a cold by being cold. The tongue has zones capable of distinguishing different flavours. Napoleon was a dwarf and George Washington had wooden teeth. Columbus discovered America, despite its several million existing residents and the various Norsemen, Phoenicians and Welsh who pipped him to the post.

# WATCH BATS

On a summer's night at 10:00, when the skies are still a light purple with hints of yellow, like a week-old blunt trauma injury, one may watch bats swooping and darting in the aethereal cauldrons formed between trees.

Bats move so quickly in the darkness that 'watching' them is something of a misnomer. One merely has a retinal impression of possible-bat. Then it is over.

### 'ARE YOU SURE THEY ARE BATS?'

Well, yes, they are certainly not swallows or swifts. The latter are tucked up in their nests by 10:00. By a process of elimination these rapacious shadows must be bats.

### 'THEY'RE CREEPY AREN'T THEY.'

My loud-voiced friend, you will scare the bats off. Yes, they are creepy. Why, is a mystery. A swift should be much more creepy, since it is further away on the evolutionary tree. A swift is a winged dinosaur: a bat is practically a relative.

### 'YES BUT IMAGINE IF ONE FLEW IN YOUR FACE OR GOT TANGLED UP IN YOUR HAIR OR BIT YOU OR LOOKED IN YOUR EYES FOR A MOMENT.'

Yes, and said something in the voice of Christopher Lee, such as 'Would you care to join me for a glass of sherry before retiring?'

# GO TO A NIGHT-DIVE

There are various sorts of club that cater to people who like to stay up late. One sort is the dancing club. Here one may swallow various preparations and find partners for off-the-cuff romance. One line you might try: 'Please kiss me.'

Another sort is the jazz club, where one sits listening to musicians who look as if they would be just as happy if you were not there. Perhaps they have headaches. Preparations and romance may not be indulged in at the tables.

A third type is the cabaret club. Here one may see performers in various media: spoken word, comedy, theatre, etc. Fishnet tights are usually worn, and may be handed out at the door.

I have little experience of any of these, but enough to say that when you get home you will count your money and swear that there is a twenty-pound note missing you can't account for. You will also have an acrid taste in the back of your mouth and a sneaking suspicion you have done something shameful in addition to the shameful things you are quite certain you have done.

LVII

# WRITE A NOVEL

Novel-writing manuals will advise you to do certain things to increase your chances of producing publishable prose. For example, publishers don't react well to writing that is ungrammatical, poorly punctuated and devoid of evident sense, as in 'I suppose theyre dead long ago the 2 of them its like all through a mist makes you feel so old I made the scones of course I had everything all to myself then a girl Hester we used to compare our hair mine was thicker than hers she showed me how to settle it at the back when I put it up and whats this else how to make a knot on a thread with the one hand we were like cousins what age was I then the night of the storm...' Except that this is an excerpt from *Ulysses*. This is of course intended to demonstrate 1) that rules are meant to be broken, 2) publishers turn down the current crop of masterpieces at a rate of about a thousand per week, 3) you can get away with anything if you are James Joyce.

Among other common novel-writing nostrums are: have an ideal reader in mind (though if you actually address that reader, you may turn into Henry Fielding); write dialogue that speaks of the characters' hidden motivations (though if you hide their motivations really effectively no one will have a clue what is happening); and delay the reader's gratification (though not to the point when they take your book back to the shop and demand a refund).

# LVIII

# MEDITATE ON YOUR MORTALITY

In a churchyard near where I live is a headstone. The inscription reads:

> This world it is a city full of crooked streets
> Death is a market place where all men meet.
> If life were Marchandice that men could buy
> Rich men would ever live and poor men die.

Yes, at the marketplace of death only one transaction is possible, and all ledgers have but one column: debit.

All around us are cities of the dead. It is instructive to look at crowd scenes in old photographs – for example Mafeking Day, 1889 – and reflect that everyone there is dead. Not one of them became immortal. Not even *one*. Not even the babies. It seems a little hard.

Hobbes called our lives 'nasty, brutish and short'. Schopenhauer developed the idea, saying: 'Life is an unpleasant business. I have resolved to spend it reflecting on it.' A third philosopher – details have yet to be filled in – could develop it still further, taking the idea to a positive conclusion: 'During my reflections on the Hobbesian and Schopenhauerian unpleasantness of life, I came to the unexpected and wonderful realisation of such-and-such.' There seems to be an opening here. I have done the spade-work.

# MEDITATE ON YOUR POSSIBLE IMMORTALITY

We are told by futurologists that the rapid pace of scientific and medical advance makes it likely that the first person to live to 200 is already alive. And surely by the time that person reaches 200 it will be easy to extend his or her life indefinitely. Mortality, like much else, is not what it was.

At night, the thought comes unbidden: what if that person is me? What if I am destined to live forever, either in this skull or a new one? Am I in the van of a new race of super-powerful immortals? For if it becomes possible to cheat death, then surely everything else becomes possible too. I will control the world entirely by my thoughts; fly without wings; see through walls (and clothes); attain eternal youth; and finally achieve the happiness that my mother promised me.

Perhaps, even if it is not my destiny to reach that exalted state, a future race of immortals with unlimited time on their hands will devote themselves to the project of resurrecting everyone who has ever been alive. A child who died of the plague in medieval Bristol, for example, surely deserves to taste a few more of life's joys.

However, if I have died by then, I wonder if I might not be a little annoyed at being plucked from a comfortable oblivion without written permission. Do-gooding can be taken too far. Did Lazarus wish to be raised? No one seems to have asked.

# LX

# STUMBLE UPON WICCAN GATHERINGS

If you walk alone at night in the woods often enough, you will stumble upon the good burghers of your town engaged in occult activity. Listen for the sounds of chickens being slaughtered. Perhaps you will catch a glimpse of white robes among the trees, or fire-illumined, nude bodies.

You can maximize your chances of seeing witches by walking in the woods around Walpurgisnacht, which falls on 30 April. Walpurgisnacht is named after St Walpurga, an English missionary much concerned with the souls of the pagan tribes of Germany. This redoubtable female, with the magnificent carriage (as I conceive her) of an early 20th-century suffragist, was in no way connected with witches, black Sabbaths or Old Harry-copulating; but the day of her canonization coincided with Germanic traditions of witches' gatherings, and the association has stuck.

In medieval times the forces that threatened human beings – disease, storms, earthquakes, famine – were often attributed to the maleficent influence of witches. Nowadays these forces have been tamed or explained, and the colour has consequently been drained from life. We are nostalgic for mystery, pain and blood. One need only stroll around a modern secular temple such as a DIY chain store to account for the resurgence of interest in Satanism.

Please reflect that the next time you buy a roll of loft insulation you are contributing to the death of an innocent fowl in a midnight glade.

## LXI

# CONTEMPLATE THE DAWN OF TIME

It is very easy to see the dawn of time: simply look up. The light from some of the faintest stars was emitted before the earth itself was even formed. That light journeyed across interstellar wastes for four billion years, finally reaching your retina. One hopes it feels it was worth the effort.

It seems that the universe is comprehensible merely by standing in the dark and looking.

Not so fast,. What underlies the phenomena we see?

Atoms, one might say. Yet Wilhelm Reich begged to differ. At the core of his life's work was his discovery of orgone energy, the primal sex-stuff of the universe. Orgone energy was not merely bioelectrical sexual energy, nor even the life force, but the essence of matter itself. Tiny particles he called 'bions' were concentrated orgone energy, and were the basic units that Democritus and Rutherford had unaccountably missed. 'Orgonotic' pulsations filled the universe, and the galaxies themselves were riotous orgone streams in space. When the body had absorbed enough of this background radiation it discharged it in the form of an orgasm; and luckily for people who like a lot of orgasms, Reich invented an 'orgone accumulator', a sort of hut made with walls of alternating organic and metallic layers, that one could sit inside to recharge.

Am I alone in finding this a more attractive explanation for the marvels we see when we observe the night sky?

# APPRECIATE YOUR OWN VASTNESS

As one looks up at the stars, one is wont to feel small. 'Our lives are so insignificant.' 'Nothing really matters very much.'

Wrong! You matter very greatly. You are as important as any galaxy.

The human scale is intermediate between the macroscopic and microscopic. At the macroscopic scale, the universe is a thousand trillion times as big as the human body. However, at the microscopic scale, the smallest particles are about a thousand trillion times as small as the human body. In terms of our position in the universe, we are intermediate: not pathetic ants at the narrow end of a telescope, utterly dwarfed by our celestial surroundings, but island universes, containing myriad cells, molecules, atoms and particles. Human beings straddle both the infinite and the infinitesimal, looking in both directions.

So the next time you look up at the stars, do not be intimidated by them.

Walt Whitman knew this:

## I am large, I contain multitudes.

The poets always get there first.

# LXIII

# LAMB

Lambing takes place at all hours. One may lamb during the day or at night. If one has goats, one may also kid.

Go on a March night. Many farms are happy to welcome visitors (especially paying ones). There is a nativity waiting for you in the winter straw, in the blood and the mucus and the night: one could imagine kings and angels attending this event. Shepherds, naturally, are already present. (If you take steps beforehand to ensure that there is no place for you at an inn, for example by insulting a publican, then the correspondences will approach fantastic levels.)

Lambs are born feet and head foremost, as if making a high dive from the womb to the world. Dumped in the straw, struggling in their amniotic sacs, unbreathing, unable to stand, they are licked into life by their mothers (or else a canny farm girl inserts a straw into a twitching nose to force a sneeze). However, in some places, lambs are aborted before they can be born naturally. These are then killed and skinned, which provides the softest leather.

Oh, humankind! Is there no crime against the animals you will not contemplate? What is more helpless, fragile, beautiful, deserving of our protection, than a just-born lamb, meek and mild?

In a trice the smell of roast meat resurrects our indifference.

# MOTH

To go collecting moths is known as mothing. Naturally one may also moth, in the present simple. A person who moths is called a mother, though the spelling may lead to confusion.

There are dozens of families of moths, and tens of thousands of species. Using light-boxes, mercury vapour lamps, phero-mone-based lures and other equipment, you may entrap and examine them. Moths, though colourless, have colourful names. They include the Mother Shipton, the Forester, the Reed Leopard, the Apple Leaf Skeletonizer, the Chimney Sweeper, the Nettle-tap, the Timothy Tortrix, the Cotoneaster Webworm, the Beautiful China-mark, the Large Tabby, the Drinker, the Dwarf Cream Wave, the Many-lined, the Geometrician, the Garden Tiger, the Blotched Emerald, the Three-humped Prominent, the Ni Moth, the Shark, the Buff Footman, the Setaceous Hebrew Character, the Pale Stigma, the L-Album Wainscot and the Old Lady.

I belong to a mothing club that meets in the school playing fields on summer nights. I find the members as fascinating as the moths. Among the interesting species I have collected are the Buff Scoutmaster, the Corduroy Fishwife, the Disillusioned Schoolteacher and the Disgraced Policeman.

# CONJURE UP THE GHOSTS
# OF ANCIENT CONQUESTS

This can be done through the expedient of taking a narcanthus bonbon. The narcanthus flower is not an aphrodisiac; rather it stimulates the linked faculties of taste and smell to evoke memories of amorous dalliance. I do not know where one can currently find narcanthus bonbons. I have a small supply for my own use from the manufacturer Giraudan of Nîmes, with the brand name '*Perles de Parnassus*'. The effect of the bonbon is very far from Parnassian, however, with that mountain's reputation for scholastic endeavour.

So: at night, when all around are snoring, take a journey into the past. Put on a smoking jacket or some other appropriate item of attire, close your eyes and place one narcanthus bonbon under your tongue. Allow it to dissolve.

What first comes to mind? In my case, the murderous nape of Ettie, that half Xunganese, half Formosan princess famous for her sly *oeillades*, never faithful, but who captivated me with her extraordinary gymnastic abilities and... but are these really my recollections, or someone else's?

Narcanthus has that effect.

# LXVI

# DO NOT GO TO A FIREWORK DISPLAY

A firework display will leave you feeling hollow inside. One should generally be wary of entertainment. Better to do something badly oneself than to see another doing it well.

Instead, set off your own fireworks. This is much more satisfying. There is a childish delight, never quite extinguishable, connected with handling little packages of explosive: the small possibility you might be blinded or deprived of fingers is intensely alluring. These cunning little rockets, bombs and squibs, with their garish colours, appeal to our most primitive urges. If fireworks could speak, they would say: 'Bring me to the pinnacle of a beautiful death.'

And the smell of fireworks, like an Icelandic breakfast. Eggs and salt, cooked in a volcano.

In these small packages are millennia of chemical wisdom. The firework is, after all, one of the four basic inventions bequeathed us by the Chinese: paper, printing, the magnetic compass and the firework. The root of civilization, and perhaps the root of our undoing: for what is a nuclear weapon but a gigantic firework?

After Guy Fawkes' Night, I wander the streets at five o'clock in the morning, picking up the spent casings ('Lucky Fountain of Eden', 'Illuminator', 'Steel Beauty'). I take them home and examine them, battered, ripped and scorched, having given their all. I press my nose deep into them, snuffing their vanished fire, imagining fires to come.

LXVII

# LEARN ABOUT THE MOTIONS
# OF THE PLANETS

Like bowels, planets have motions. They are 'wandering stars'. Any fool can learn the names of the fixed stars: over there is the Pole Star; over there is Betelgeuse; etc. But what is that shocking yellow blob in Orion? It wasn't there last week. It could be Venus, certainly, but it could equally be Jupiter, or Saturn, or Mars. They all look roughly the same. Where did it come from, and where is it going next? This is true intellectual enquiry; 'the rest is stamp-collecting'.

The ancients recognised five planets: Mercury, Venus, Mars, Jupiter and Saturn. These are the naked-eye planets. Uranus, Neptune and Pluto, the clothed-eye planets, are too faint to see, and were only discovered in recent centuries. (The discoverer of Uranus originally named it 'George's Star', after George III, which is simultaneously obsequious and inaccurate, since it is not a star: but perhaps he didn't think the king would care. Its eventual name, Uranus, commemorates the father of Aphrodite, who engendered her when Zeus cut his testicles off and threw them into the ocean: the froth from his testicles gave rise to his daughter.)

The five naked-eye planets wander around the heavens with scant regard for propriety: occasionally they stop, reverse direction, then think better of it and resume their course. Attempting to account for the motions of the planets precipitated humankind into science, and thus into the world we experience today. If there were no planets there would be no plumbing, polyester or Prozac.

94

# WRITE AN ENTRY IN YOUR DIARY

I believe it was Oscar Wilde who said that he always took his diary with him because it gave him something sensational to read on the train. Well, Oscar led a highly colourful life. Many rented youths from Clerkenwell could attest to that fact. However, you need not lead a colourful life to write a colourful diary. There are infinite riches in a little room, as Pascal put it, or John Donne, or perhaps Shakespeare.

I personally favour the one-sentence diary. In this, there is no self-imposed obligation to produce a narrative: one may simply produce an impression, a psychic summary, a night-reflection, that will be more revealing, when one comes to read it in future years, than any mere daytime-shopping-list of events. Something that is rich, dense, livid with existence. April 3rd: 'The skin of my face is grey and pitted: there is no disguising how much I have deteriorated.' May 19th: 'Ah, the youth of old trees.' June 23rd: 'The sound of a door slamming as someone goes out while you remain at home, with nothing to do, is one of the most melancholy of all sounds, especially when, after the slam, the house relapses into a deep, unbroken silence, almost like a sleep.'

If you open the diary and your mind is a blank, you can just write 'My mind is a blank,' and snap it shut. Currently, fifteen of my entries for this month take that form.

# LXIX

# LEAF THROUGH OLD PHOTOGRAPH ALBUMS

The photograph album is becoming a thing of the past. Most people keep their photographs in computers. This is utter folly. One solar storm, one modest atomic explosion, and they will all be destroyed forever. And not just our photographs but our music and our literature. Thus the jpeg, the mp3 and the e-book are handmaidens of our cultural apocalypse.

Compare the experience of leafing through photograph albums, slightly mouldy and musty and water-stained, assembled in remote ages – the past is a foreign country, they develop film differently there – with the experience of scrolling, bored, and with a tiny headache, through a mass of ever-bright jpegs, bmps, gifs and pngs, and you will, I hope, understand my position.

Please spend this night in the following way: print out all of your vulnerable computer-images, and then stick them in a series of old-fashioned albums. When your computer malfunctions or you die or your house is repossessed or you go insane, the albums will still be there to be enjoyed and pored over by future generations, who, after laughing at your fashion sense and facial hair, will peer seriously into your eyes and wonder what manner of man you were, what loves, what greeds, what griefs.

# FEED HEDGEHOGS

Hedgehogs may be fed a variety of foodstuffs: dog or cat food, chopped boiled eggs, meat scraps. The only thing they may not be fed is the one thing that tradition says they should be fed, i.e. bread soaked in milk. This follows the rule that everything you know is wrong, which is usually right. Bread and milk will give a hedgehog diarrhoea, and there is little worse than hedgehog diarrhoea on your lawn.

If you put out food, and watch your garden throughout the night – a tedious recreation, I will admit – you may notice that a particular hedgehog will begin to visit regularly. You might go so far as to name this hedgehog 'Spiny', 'Spiky', 'Sonic', 'Mrs Tiggy-Winkle', or 'Harry', and fondly imagine that it is your own. But in fact, a large number of hedgehogs may detect the presence of boiled eggs and visit your hog-table, and so 'Spiny' or 'Sonic' may be one of several hedgehogs masquerading as the same animal. All hedgehogs look alike to the untrained eye. The situation is rather like the Walt Disney films in which a single animal is represented by several dozen animals that are taken behind the set and mercilessly killed when they no longer resemble the Platonic animal the director has in mind.

# LXXI

# MAKE A CROP CIRCLE

In the heyday of crop circles, there was quite serious discussion about their origins: as alien artefacts, as manifestations of wind-vortices, as messages from spiritual intelligences. Then two unspiritual-looking middle-aged chaps turned up with a couple of planks and explained how they'd fooled the world. To create a simple circle, you simply secured a plank by ropes from your shoulders, and, extending it like a plane's rudder-board, moved in a circle, flattening grain as you went, moving gradually inwards. Hey presto! The mystery was solved.

Not at all. Just because something is debunked, it doesn't mean that people stop believing in it. And after all, could this barbaric plank-method *really* account for the most complex designs? The ones featuring Mandelbrot sets and fractal octohedra? More middle-aged chaps came forward, this time equipped with laser sighting equipment and PhDs. But could this *really* account...? The iterations were endless, like the Mandelbrot set itself.

Perhaps you will wish to contribute to the genre: if so, night is your essential ally. Night enables you to execute your designs without coming to the attention of sceptics, or, more importantly, farmers. The true opponent of the cerealogist is not the disbeliever but the man with the shotgun.

If you are abducted while making your circle, farmers may be responsible.

LXXII

# READ A GIDEON'S BIBLE

Gideon, after whom the Gideon's Bible is named, was asked by God to separate his men prior to battle. Here is the text, from my own Gideon's:

> So he brought down the people unto the water: and the LORD said unto Gideon, Every one that lappeth of the water with his tongue, as a dog lappeth, him shalt thou set by himself; likewise every one that boweth down upon his knees to drink. And the number of them that lapped, putting their hand to their mouth, were three hundred men: but all the rest of the people bowed down upon their knees to drink water. And the LORD said unto Gideon, By the three hundred men that lapped will I save you, and deliver the Midianites into thine hand: and let all the other people go every man unto his place.

Are you a kneeler or a lapper? I am an unapologetic kneeler. This means I do not have to fight the Midianites, and can instead 'go unto my place', i.e. my flat in town.

Biblical exegesis is an absorbing pastime. Try it: who knows? You may make a major theological discovery. Delve deeply into the text. Follow the example of Origen, the 3rd-century exegete and author of the *Hexapla*, who had seven secretaries to record the wisdom that ceaselessly dripped from his beard, and who claimed that each Biblical verse could be interpreted on three levels: literal, moral and allegorical.

However, do not follow Origen's example too devotedly. On the strength of a verse in Matthew, he is believed to have 'made himself a eunuch for the kingdom of heaven'.

# LXXIII

# MAKE A FAUSTIAN PACT

The strange thing about Faust was his lack of ambition. He asked for a mere twenty-three years of dalliance with Helen, after which Mephistopheles could do what he liked with him. Surely Faust should have asked for a thousand years, or ten thousand. The devil, living in eternity, does not care how protracted your enjoyment is, as long as your soul finally becomes his property.

Then again, ten thousand years still end, and they never end well. 'See, see, how Christ's blood streams in the firmament!' A shame. But that is the nature of the pact. Jam today, damnation tomorrow.

I have no experience in summoning up Satan. I imagine it is done roughly like this. Buy a pig's head from your local butcher and mount it on a stake in your bedroom. Draw a seven-sided mandala on the floor, sit inside it, light some black candles and recite the Lord's prayer backwards before invoking the Unholy Name: 'Oh Lucifer, I renounce God and all the saints, I bow down before you, your faithful supplicant and slave.' You may add here: 'and please help me get my child back from social services' or 'and please find my keys'. You may notice a vile stench at this point.

For Green Satanists, a tofu pig's head can be bought from a little shop in Covent Garden I know.

# HOLD A SÉANCE

Naturally one need not go the whole hog, or even part of the hog (its head).

A perfectly blameless séance is possible, in which the Devil is far away from your thoughts. (Of course, you still may not be far away from *His* thoughts.)

Gather together a like-minded group of people, making sure that there are no skeptics among your number, since derisive laughter tends to put spirits off. A group of six people is excellent, since it is twice the magic number of three. In the room, light six candles (white ones: why tempt fate?), and convene at a round table. In the centre of the table put a ouija board: all should then place their fingers on the central glass, and one among you call the spirits with a formula such as: 'Spirits of the dead, we entreat you to make your presence known to us, humble students of the infinite.' Then ask a question that the spirit can spell out the answer to, for example: 'Are you there?' Do not ask: 'What is the capital of Burkina Faso?'

You may find it politic to recruit a medium for the session. Mediums are listed in the yellow pages, and the best are members of the Professional League of Arcanists, Spiritualists and Mediums (PLASM). Like house-buyers seeking conveyancing, spirits appreciate an expert.

# LXXV

# IMPRISON A CRICKET
# IN A CAGE

First, as Mrs Beeton might have said in an entomological moment, catch your cricket. This is best done during the day, when crickets are visible in long grass. Steal up to her and, with a cupped hand, pounce. Put her in a teacup.

Next fashion a tiny cage from wire. Wire can be bought from any hardware shop. You will also need a soldering iron and a round metal plate – try a lid from a large jar – to act as a base. Take care that the bars are closely spaced to prevent escape. Then transfer your cricket into the cage and set it on a table, or suspend it from the ceiling. At night, especially if you dim the lights, the cricket will begin to chirp, evoking memories of a rustic childhood spent among pot-bellied farmers and their wives, a life of ferreting, mangolds and pig-nuts.

Hold on, though. Is it entirely moral to incarcerate one of God's creatures purely for your entertainment? Ha ha. Moral? I would ask you to look around you. The gloss on the cover of this book is made from sheep lymph. Rabbits are killed to grow muesli. The cricket is symbolic of your complicity in the suffering of the brutes. In fact, that is the doleful meaning of her song. Can you listen, and nod your head, and let a tear escape from your eye, listen without releasing her?

# LXXVI

# TALK TO STREET SWEEPERS

In the very early hours of the morning, street sweepers are the only people awake. They ride in their little fat machines, whirring over the detritus, making the streets new for the morrow. They are snug inside there: wrapped up warm, headphones on, navigating through their personal ocean of broken glass and free newspapers. There is no need for them to emerge.

Except if you stop them with a hand.

'I can see you are busy,' you say, 'but I wanted to ask you something, if you wouldn't mind. Yes, if you wouldn't mind taking off your headphones. What do you think about people who carelessly drop litter? Do you ever drop litter yourself? Do you enjoy your work? How long have you been doing this job? Is the pay good? What is your earliest memory? Yes, it is relevant, I assure you. What is waste? Philosophically speaking. Is waste a neurosis? Did your mother ever hunt through your bedroom wastebasket, looking for secrets? If you see a pair of knickers in the gutter do you stop and collect it by hand? Yes, you may ask me any question you like. Oh, that question. Well, I suppose I don't fuck off because I prefer to stay here. Very well. Yes, you may proceed. Yes, that is very clear. Yes.'

# HAVE A BONFIRE

What is the origin of the word bonfire? It looks suspiciously like Norman French: a 'good fire'. I suppose in those far-off days there must have been two types of fire, the bonfire and the malfire.

A question: why don't people have bonfires during the day? It would be a poor show; almost pointless. Only at night does the bonfire acquire significance. Imagine! For countless generations this was the only source of illumination, warmth and safety. It was light bulb, central heating, cooking range, locked door and television all rolled into one.

Is there such a thing as an ancestral memory? Is it possible that past epochs really do reach into us with gnarled fingers? That is the heresy of Lamarck, if I am not mistaken. Expose a child to bonfires for three hundred generations and the three hundred and first will respond with delighted approval. All nonsense, I am told. And yet it cannot be. Stare into those embers and tell me you do not see childbirth and war, pain and love and woe and death there. The glow on sweaty faces, smeared with grease. Roasting meat on long sticks. Wine, Wicca and song! Tell me you do not feel a strange spell being cast, do not sense this message, or something like it: 'Your mother's mother's mother looked into me and felt as you feel, as will your daughter's daughter's daughter.'

# SKETCH SHADOWS

A drawing begins with a line, delineating an object. That object is situated in a milieu, containing objects similarly delineated. The result? A scene conceived as if perfectly lit, with all its outlines distinct, a day-scene, in fact.

Pens and pencils are the problem. These produce lines. What one wants is something that produces not lines, but masses.

Choose instead, therefore, a brush or a stick of charcoal. Now something changes. One's focus shifts. One can sketch in blocks, swathes, pools. This is ideally suited to the capture of shadows[1], and thus night-scenes.

Caravaggio was an artist of the dark; as were Goya, Daumier and Bacon. The greatest of all artists of the dark, however, was Kazimir Malevich. A number of his Suprematist canvases are entirely black. They have not even the relief of a signature. They are simultaneously the negation of the sketch and its greatest apotheosis, since they may be considered portraits of any and all objects. 'My aunt, unillumined.' 'Bedford on a moonless night.' 'The absence that failed to make the heart grow fonder.' Etc.

---

1 Who may also have been a firm of solicitors.

# EXAMINE YOUR SHELVES FOR BOOKS YOU HAVE NOT READ

Sort your books into two collections, one read and the other unread. You may find that the unread collection is greater than the read. It is in my case. I have not read *Sybil* by Benjamin Disraeli. Nor have I read *Practical Pig Keeping* by Jessie Urquhart. Nor *The Virgin Book of Cocktails* by Anon. Yet all of these volumes appear on my shelves. Perhaps one day I will relax by my sty with a Kir Royale in one hand and Disraeli in the other, but it seems unlikely.

Even more surprising are brand-new books: examine your unread collection and you will almost certainly find some that have been bought new and never once opened. These may be set aside as possible gifts, since you obviously feel disinclined to read them. However, some books are impossible to give as presents. One would need a very sure hand to give Conrad's *Heart of Darkness*, or anything by Samuel Beckett: these would cast a damper on any christening.

In fact, it is a salutary exercise to count the books one has actually read during one's lifetime. In my case the total is in the low tens. The others I have merely heard of. Some books that I have written I have not read. The two activities are, after all, distinct.

# INVENT A LANGUAGE

English is a serviceable enough language. A language that could capably chart the surface of an alien world, as it has conquered half of this one. Often a beautiful language. Nevertheless something is missing. English wears its heart on its sleeve. There is no evasion, ambiguity, or deception in it. It is strangely monotone. It is a language to inspire, to command, to explain, but never to deepen the mystery of the world.

For this, you should spend the darkling hours inventing your own language; and when the day breaks, go out and inflict it on the public. Use only a few words, perhaps no more than 200. They will soon catch on. Use associations of nouns to create vocabulary: so, for example, if fire is *woff* and stick is *hruurr*, then a match would be a *woff-hruurr*; and if number is *filltip* and machine is *slaughterballs*, then a calculator would be a *filltip-slaughterballs*. Give some thought to matters such as the position of verbs, how many vowels to have, how many consonants, how (and whether) you indicate plurals, how (and whether) you indicate gender, how you form questions, and not a few other things.

Speaking in an invented language has many benefits, one of which is that if you answer the phone with a courteous 'Humash fruhlingspikka wartnerbish khong-khoxx monkeyfroth?' ('God give you good day and how may I serve you?') then people calling about PPI fraud will hang up immediately.

# LXXXI

# DREAM LUCIDLY

For too long, your dreams have dreamed you. Now it is time for you to dream them.

Start by developing a habit such as this: during your everyday waking life, count off the fingers of one hand. Do this repeatedly, several times a day, until it becomes a habit.

Soon this habit will make its way into your dreaming life. You will begin to dream that you are counting your fingers. However, in the dream, something will be subtly wrong. Perhaps you will have six fingers, like Anne Boleyn. Or perhaps your fingers will blur together. At this moment, in the dream, you will realise you are dreaming. This is the trigger. Possessed of self-knowledge of your mental state, you will now be able to take control. Your dream will become 'lucid'. The joystick is yours: where do you wish to go?

Actually, for many people, the question is not so much where do you wish to go, but who do you wish to have sex with first. However, I will assume that you are above such considerations. You may wish to heal lepers, witness the signing of the Treaty of Versailles, or talk to Leonardo da Vinci. Suffice it to say that once you begin to dream lucidly, you will be able to take part in whatever fantasy your imagination can devise. There will be no British Board of Film Classification to interfere.

# WATCH BADGERS

It tends to be persons who dislike and fear badgers who see them the most; so, if you want to spot badgers, go on a walk with someone who is actively trying to avoid them.

If you cannot find such a person, you may have to pursue other methods. The best way to maximise your chances is to scout in woodland for suitable badger sites. These tend to be on sloping ground, since badgers, living underground, prefer to dig horizontally rather than vertically. The heaps of spoil will give you a clue as to the locations of the setts.

Badgers are nocturnal, emerging after dusk to forage. Take up a position some way from the sett, downwind. You should probably not try to interact with the badgers: they are wild animals, and will not hesitate to maim you. Confine yourself to observing them from a distance, perhaps with a pair of night-vision binoculars.

In former times, badger-baiting was a popular sport, although I am unsure as to what exactly it involved. It almost certainly did not consist of tying a badger to the end of a line and lowering it into water to catch fish. Instead it probably involved using specially-trained dogs to attack badgers and rip them to shreds. When the fun was over the men would kick the shreds moodily and then go home, obscurely dissatisfied with their lot.

# LXXXIII

# CREATE A BOUDOIR

What is a boudoir? Well, it is the French for bedroom. However, a French boudoir is a rather more sophisticated zone than an English bedroom. A French boudoir is a place that an Englishman or Englishwoman might well find difficult to comprehend, being, as it is, the arena of a peculiarly Continental celebration of the body, its smells and exudations, a place where one gasps on pillows of roseate flesh, where outlandish cries are torn from unwilling throats, and where the pleasures of the hour are absolved by that other typically Gallic contrivance, the bidet, a species of watery Confessional. Nevertheless.

A boudoir – very well, let us say bedroom: there is no need to submit ourselves so cravenly, as long as we know exactly what we are talking about – should be a place of relaxation and intimacy, where the senses are gently stimulated. There should be nothing harsh or jarring: no sharp angles or metallic colours. All must be soft and, yes, let us say it, feminine. Golds, oranges, browns. Not too many blues or greens, suggesting, as they do, the sky and sea, realms of masculine endeavour. Fabrics, that, in the flickering of candles, will enhance by their reflected light the hues of flesh. On the floor, animal skins. On the shelves, books bound in mottled leather. On the walls, engravings depicting Asiatic scenes, in which slave-girls splash petulantly in pools as they await their master, a young vizier prematurely enfeebled by their caresses, no longer fit for statecraft or war, but only mindless sensual indulgence.

# LXXXIV

# REJECT THE SENSUALITY
# OF THE FRENCH

Alternatively you may wish to design your bedroom in such a way that even the name 'bedroom' is too carnal, containing as it does the slightly disreputable word 'bed'.

A bedroom considered in this way rejects entirely the French exaltation of the flesh. Gone are the rich fabrics, books, pictures, rugs and other decorations: instead is only the brutality, severity and honesty of wood, stone and plaster. Such a room is nothing less than a monastic cell, a place for repose, certainly, but only between bouts of self-mortification. If there is a carpet it is worn by the tread of many sinful feet (not that they were doing anything sinful in here, I can assure you); and in fact there is nothing in this room to suggest it is even yours; it is anonymous. Iron bedstead, thin bedclothes, wax candles, and perhaps a plain ceramic ewer for laving oneself with, set in a priedieu of medieval sternness. In summary, a veritable madhouse of self-denial.

In this way will you atone for the sins of your fellow men, who are even now, as you kneel to beg for forgiveness, engaged in shameless materialistic practices such as 'shopping', 'watching television' and 'going to work'.

# LEARN A MUSICAL INSTRUMENT

Nothing is guaranteed to get up the neighbours' noses more than practising a musical instrument at three in the morning. If you hate your neighbours, therefore, do this.

However, if you are not as hate-filled as I give you credit for, various soundless methods can be employed. One version is the electronic keyboard. This can be fitted with headphones so that the noise you make audible only to you. (However you should make sure you are not, in the throes of musical ecstasy, inadvertently making groaning noises à la Oscar Peterson.)

Another option is the electric guitar, which may also be fitted with headphones. An electric guitar without amplification is essentially silent: it will not penetrate through brick and plaster.

A third option is the gamelan orchestra. Perhaps you have a gamelan orchestra in your home. The instruments of the gamelan are traditionally 'damped' using the left hand; after each note is struck with the right, the player touches the key with the left to prevent the sound ringing out too fully.

The greatest disturbance connected with the gamelan orchestra is the chatter and clatter of the gamelan musicians themselves as they tramp into and around your home in the small hours, and the smells of their cooking.

# CONTEMPLATE SHADOWS

Modern life seeks to eliminate shadows. Under the glare of an electric bulb all dirt and disease are exposed and eliminated. Like a sadistic guard interrogating a prisoner, the Enlightenment, which gave us electricity and hygiene, turned a spotlight full in the face of Mother Nature. Fair enough. I, for one, have no wish to contract cholera, and so I reluctantly yield up Mother Nature to be probed and screamed at. But what have we lost?

Shadows. Candlelight. Interiors with gradations of light and darkness. Dusky regions, even in one's own rooms, where no light ever penetrates. Subtlety. Imagination is powerfully drawn to those things that the eyes cannot see. Remove shadow and we remove mystery. Remove shadow and we remove anticipation of delight or horror.

Why else our forebears' obsession with gold, if not for the fact that gold can absorb the tiniest bit of candlelight and glow warmly in even the most gloom-enshrouded interior?

When Rembrandt's picture *The Night Watch* was cleaned, it was found that the 'Night' was in reality dirt, and the painting was actually set in broad daylight. The chiaroscuro for which the painter was famed was nothing more than a patina of smut and grease. And with that smut and grease gone, all the magic of the canvas was lost. Tourists pass by it with nary a glance, and its postcards languish in the racks.

# TELEPHONE

When was the last time you got a telephone call in the small hours? It never happens. No one rings anyone at night – except in films, of course – because it is a generally agreed fact that the only possible reason for a night-time call is a death. A small-hours call means death *at the minimum*, and perhaps something even more serious, such as multiple death, earthquake, tsunami or revolution.

A person who picks up the phone at night is therefore in a uniquely vulnerable position, half awake and at the same time stricken with a nameless dread, like a librarian in a tale by HP Lovecraft. Such is the gravity of the night-time phone call that any statement is believable. Try it: pick a number at random from the phone book and announce to the person who answers: 'The money is under the Audi outside.' (There will usually be an Audi outside.) Hang up before they can ask 'What money?' This will plunge them into an agony of speculation about being under surveillance by mafiosi.

Or: 'The guards are coming for me now. I only wanted to say I love you. Goodbye forever.' This may elicit a strangled scream of 'Monica!'

Of course, you should never really do this: it is sheer sadism.

# SET OFF CHINESE FIRE LANTERNS

It is astonishing that fire lanterns are not prohibited: recently, near where I live, a fire lantern set a barn alight, severely burning a cat, which had to go about for weeks with bandaged paws. And these little *cosmoi* of paper, wire and wax are a serious threat to aircraft. Imagine one being sucked into a jet engine; imagine the damage it could do, the resulting catastrophic loss of control, screams, overturned drinks trolleys, etc.

The only really safe place to set off a fire lantern is from the deck of a ship in the open ocean far away from any known airlanes. Since you are unlikely to be in this position very often, when you find yourself at sea you should set off a good few to get the whole thing out of your system.

Alternatively you could go to northern Thailand in November, where there is a Buddhist festival called Yi Peng. At Yi Peng, celebrants set off thousands of fire lanterns at once in the name of the Buddha, and then watch as they swarm and struggle into the night sky like angry jellyfish. You can join in without scruple. After all, if everyone else is doing something wrong, it ceases in any meaningful way to be wrong. Doesn't it?

# LXXXIX

# LISTEN TO THE SAD STRAINS OF AN AEOLIAN HARP

The Aeolian harp, as we know, is a device consisting of a sounding-box wound with catgut or similar fibre, which, when placed in a breeze – a mild zephyr is sufficient – emits a strange, ethereal sound, like distant fairies encouraging other distant fairies at a football match. The notes constantly change as the breeze brushes one or another of the strings, and by some unexplained mechanism the sound produced is always in much higher registers than the actual tuning of the strings themselves. A mystery, one which I would be very miserable to see solved.

The poet Coleridge was a devotee of the Aeolian harp: he even penned an ode to it. The birth of Romanticism is very much tied up with this instrument: play on harp-strings and you play on heart-strings. Every poet of the period would have an Aeolian harp on his windowsill, even in the meanest garret. If he neglected to do so he would be sure to attract the disapproving looks of other visiting consumptives.

On a summer's night, an Aeolian harp can be a wonderful companion. It is not music in addition to, and extraneous to, the night: it is the very music *of* the night, produced by the night itself; and lost, mournful, strange, unlike any human creation.

# ATTEND A FIGHT CLUB

This may seem like a surprising thing to recommend. It may be, however, that readers hanker after violence; and fight clubs - convocations of people who wish to trade blows with one another - to my knowledge, are held at night.

So: after you have listened for long enough to your Aeolian harp, written enough letters to your future self, or gazed at the moon to satiety, you may wish to attack people with your bare hands. In other words: after the contemplative, the active.

If the infliction of physical violence seems unworthy of a thinking person, I would refer you to the words of Friedrich Nietzsche, who addressed his nearest and dearest thus:

> To those human beings who are of any concern to me I wish suffering, desolation, sickness, ill-treatment, indignities: I have no pity for them, because I wish them the only thing that can prove today whether one is worth anything or not - that one endures.

That should remove any lingering doubts. So on with your white collar, and down to Vinnie's Gym at 3am, topped up with the Teutonic Will to Power (I have a prior engagement). For extra fortification, another passage from Nietzsche:

> Who can attain to anything great if he does not feel in himself the force and will to inflict great pain? The ability to suffer is a small matter: in that line, weak women and even slaves often attain masterliness. But not to perish from internal distress and doubt when one inflicts great suffering and hears the cry of it - that is great, that belongs to greatness.

# GO NAKED NIGHT SWIMMING

The great thing about swimming naked at night is that no one can see. 'The scrotum-tightening sea' as Joyce unshrinkingly called it. (Not my friend Joyce, who coincidentally also made the same observation on holiday with me in Norfolk – I mean the Irish writer.)

Mixed naked bathing is common in various cultures around the world. Of course the secret of a pleasant experience is to plan in advance. A relaxing drink at lakeside or shore, a balmy summer's night – and then leading by personal example. Announce your intention to strip off, retreat to a respectful distance, divest yourself of your clothing and then plunge in. From the safety of the water, encourage others to follow. If they refuse, accept their refusal with good grace. (Not Grace, the friend with whom I spent that summer in Budleigh Salterton; that would be unlikely, since she abhorred nudity.)

The cool unknown of a lake on an August night, with no clothes on, the freedom, the exhilaration of it: this is the closest one can come to being a child again.

XCII

# GO TO A FIRE FESTIVAL

The Celts were devotees of night and fire. Their four great yearly ceremonies, with their sonorous names – Imbolc, Beltane, Lughnasadh and Samhain – featured colossal bonfires, roasting oxen and excess of all kinds. Very good. As Blake informs us, 'The road of excess leads to the palace of wisdom'. Of course it may also lead to the palace of justice and the house of correction.

The great Celtic night-festivals are still celebrated in many parts of these Isles. Edinburgh, for example, holds a fire festival in April on Calton Hill, with much celebration of the Death and Rebirth of the Green Man. Glastonbury, Lewes and Brighton host flamboyant parties to drive away the darkness.

But are these celebrants pagans still? Under that green body paint is the editor of the local paper, surely? The hare-head-wearer, judging by her figure, must be the postmistress. And there, that devil holding two sputtering torches, is the councillor who knocked on your door last week and asked earnestly for your opinion on energy efficiency.

These are not pagans in the guise of pillars of the community; they are pillars of the community in the guise of pagans. An important difference. If only these revellers would have the courage to sacrifice an animal and drink its blood.

# XCIII

# RIDE ON A DESERTED MERRY-GO-ROUND

In 1952 the travelling folk who supplied fairground entertainments were more trusting. They went to bed, drunk, without bothering to take elementary precautions. It was a simple matter to mount a griffin, and then, at the pull of a lever, start the whole thing rotating, to the accompaniment of the popular tunes of the day.

In 1952 life was simpler. It was understood that once the noise eventually woke the carousel's swarthy guardians they would have the right to pursue and punish. Which they did. But the beauty of a merry-go-round is that it is relatively easy to dismount from while in operation. (A waltzer would have been a different matter.) Most escaped. Harry, however, who was training for the Bar and whose father was the rector, was caught and given a severe beating. He was also later thrashed by his father, a stern man who believed that 'Unto those who hath, even more shall be given', as we read in the New Testament.

You are only young once. Having said that, you are also only old once.

XCIV

# LISTEN TO NIGHT-
# SINGING BIRDS

Nightingales or night-jars. These are not always easy to hear, but if one wanders long enough in the dark, one finds them.

The nightingale has one of the most complex of all songs: rather like a blackbird in tone, but with much greater inventiveness and at much greater length, featuring a seemingly inexhaustible repertoire of gurgles, clicks, wheeps and a characteristic two-note alternating churr, like a starter-motor repeatedly failing to bring an engine to life.

The nightjar is another chap entirely: his song is a long, rattling affair, like a clockwork toy, rising and falling with an unattractive mindlessness.

The nightingale and the nightjar are two very unlikely night-bedfellows. If they ever met, it would be like a duke meeting a mop salesman. It would be a polite encounter, certainly, but they wouldn't tarry long in one another's company. The nightingale might buy a mop: *noblesse oblige*.

And of course there are owls. Of owls I can recommend the tawny, the long-eared, the barn and the little. They are all excellent owls.

Of the songs of owls town-dwellers now know little: owls used to be present in the suburbs, but now have fled.

# READ OLD SCHOOL EXERCISE BOOKS AND DIARIES

It is said that the human body renews itself completely every seven years. In twenty-one years one has thus been renewed three times, and in thirty-five seven times. If one reaches the age of seventy, one has been renewed a total of ten times, and the renewal process has taken a terrible toll: all that renewing has left one feeling utterly debilitated.

Of course, cells are simply being copied and replaced. One does not in reality change.

Or does one? Am I still the teenager who wrote in these exercise books? I examine my painfully rounded handwriting, made with many a grunt of exertion, and wonder. The books are redolent above all of one thing: slavery to another's edicts. The scrawled figures of goblins and spaceships are islands of self-assertion in a swamp of uniforms, lunches and conformity.

Or one may read old diaries. I will predict for you one quality yours have: seriousness. Few people keep comedic diaries.

However, you must forgive your own self-absorption. To look with a forgiving eye on one's past self is an intelligent, as well as an empathetic act.

# GO TO THE CINEMA

Many cinemas have midnight film screenings. Patrons come in from the dark, then sit in the dark, and then return to the dark. The returning to the dark is as important as the coming in from the dark, because there are few more depressing experiences than seeing a film and then going back out into broad daylight.

Apparently in China a special room has been devised which is so perfectly soundproofed that the only noises perceptible are those of one's own bodily processes: the pumping of the blood, digestion, breath. Naturally this is a form of torture. Few people survive the room with their sanity intact. A cinema is the opposite. The self is decanted out. What is projected onto the screen is not the film, but the self. That is why cinemas are survivable.

At night, the cinema is only sparsely attended: perhaps only a few cineastes with their popcorn and the contents of their pockets. A subdued munching and abrasion. The plush silence, darkness, and then the gargantuan disappointment of the film itself.

Disappointment on a grand scale is what good cinema is all about. A truly satisfying work of art, at this level of immersion, would make re-entry into reality so spiritually devastating that one would be unlikely to recover. Much better to emerge from a screening and declare bitterly to one's friend: 'That was the worst nonsense I have ever seen in my life.'

# XCVII

# CULL THE SNAIL
# POPULATION

One needn't kill snails: there is always the possibility that they are reincarnations of dead ancestors. What your ancestors did to be reincarnated as snails can never be known: perhaps they were unkind to snails.

They must be got rid of somehow, though. Snails will eat most things in the garden that humans also like to eat: beans, lettuce, cabbage, etc. And it is a fact that snails come out at night to do their nefarious work. Step out with a torch past midnight, and you will see them there, discreditably feeding.

One approach is to encourage them into next door's garden, a method used by the squeamish and unprincipled: but snails are like miniskirts, periodically coming back. It has been calculated that snails need to be placed at least 100 yards away to become disorientated enough never to return, and it is quite difficult to throw a snail 100 yards. I have heard of a snail-mortar, a small tube worked by compressed spring: the snail is inserted into the tube, the desired location chosen, and the lever pressed. That is a bourne from which few snail-travellers return. Though perhaps the force of the landing sees to that.

No, the best method is to load all the snails into a bucket, drive out into the country and say farewell to them there. They will make other lives and careers for themselves, and the wrench is not so great, since each carries his own house.

# XCVIII

# WRITE LETTERS

Electronic communication is so soulless. And, as with electronic storage in general, it is extremely vulnerable to loss. One cannot keep emails tied up with a ribbon in a shoebox, though doubtless there are companies who are able to supply an 'e-shoebox' and 'e-ribbon'.

Letters have a smell. Not anything necessarily as obvious as perfume. Cream laid paper smells chalky, like a child's first lost milk-teeth; blue airmail paper smells like the vaguely stuffy contents of a grandmother's drawers. Ink has a smell, perhaps of gall or rotten wood: the great inks of the Far East are as prized for their smells as their staining qualities, and the calligraphers of those regions inhale them with nostrils as discerning and as tremulous as the great viniculturalists of France inhale a Petrus or a Domaine Leroy Mazis-Chambertin Grand Cru. It is also possible that a watermark has a smell: perhaps of water.

Letters have adjuncts. There is the stamp, for example. Many people I admire collect stamps, as do I: imitation is the sincerest form of philately. Then there are postmarks, the study of which is known as 'marcophily'. The adherents of marcophily are known as marcophiles. The postmark is essentially a form of stamp-deflowering.

A letter has personality: it instigates drama. What malice can be compacted into a flowing signature! What authority into a letterhead!

# IC

# BE DUMB

Whatever one can do speaking, one can also do unspeaking. Take the most ostensibly unlikely example – making a speech. This can be done silently through pictures and gestures. Or making a phone call. Some interlocutors are very solicitous when confronted with silence. 'I'm sorry, I didn't catch that. If you wish to hear your balance, please say "Yes". OK. Let's pass you over to customer services.'

One other thing that you can do silently is to have a meal with friends. This is known as a 'dumb supper'. These practices go back to ancient times, when people offered food to spirits in the hope that they would offer some small word of advice or refrain from causing death or illness. The various dumb supper traditions all have a flavour of the occult. In the black-and-white dumb supper, the food is either black or white in colour – white rice, black liquorice, white ice-cream, black onions, etc. – and the guests dress in black and white costumes and sit at a table covered by a black tablecloth with white napkins. In the backwards dumb supper, everything is reversed: the knives and forks are switched from left to right, the head of the house is placed at the middle of the table, and the courses are served backwards, beginning with cigars and brandy and ending with prawn cocktails. If at some point something untoward happens, such as a guest choking on a prawn cocktail or a mouse plummeting from a light-fitting, this is taken as a communication from the spirit-world and there is general pandemonium, screaming, running and trampling.

# C

# SPEND THE NIGHT IN A HAUNTED HOUSE

All houses are haunted. It is just a case of one's sensitivity. I am told that in this very house where I live, in the eighteenth century, a debased doctor murdered his clients and then sold their bodies to the medical schools. I have not personally seen his ghost, though my neighbour has. The experience so unsettled her that she now drinks constantly.

All landscapes are haunted. One may see a column of Roman soldiers tramping along the Devil's Dyke in the Hope Valley, for example. Perhaps you are bold enough (or foolish enough) to spend a night in the Screaming Woods of Long Crendon, Oxfordshire. Or see the place by the abandoned railway line where the Watercress Woman was beaten to death. Nowadays bagged salads have taken her trade.

All cities are haunted. In the alley behind my flat, in 1321, a wretched bedraggled beggar expired, and was given a pauper's funeral. So say the records in my local church.

And all churches, synagogues and temples are haunted. So many plague victims were buried in one of the boneyards nearby that the ground is even now permanently raised, a tell of human matter, causing the church to seem sunken.

Go back far enough, even, and the ghosts of dinosaurs roam the streets, bellowing despondently.

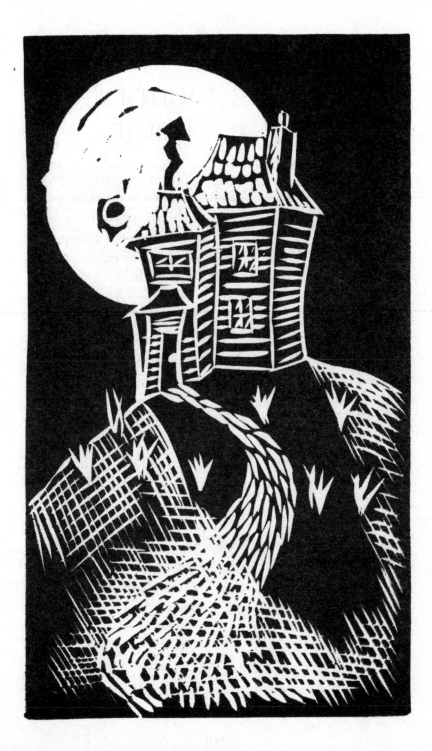

# GO OUT IN A CANOE

...into the centre of a lake, and look at the stars.

Recline on your thin skin of bark. That is the human project: a membrane of culture against the black vastness of nature. Nature indifferent below you, nature indifferent above you, and in the centre, humanity: you. How essential is man! Without the organizing genius of the human brain, all this water and sky would be a mere trash of atoms.

Swans may approach you. They recognise your superiority. 'God gave man dominion over all the beasts.' How they would love to spend time in a workshop with a lathe, fashioning a canoe. But they are simply not up to the job.

In the lapping, lilting dark, let your hand trail over the side and into the black and frigid water. Struck like a gong, the lake would ring.

It is a watery world we live in. We are told that one day the water will overwhelm us; but surely we will survive in the higher places. Islands of culture will continue. When Venice is underwater, the campanile of St Mark's Square will poke out of the flood: and in the bell-tower, in a double bed hung with magnificent brocades, the last Italian man and woman will make love energetically.

*Ha! I give you a baby!*

# CII

# GO TO SLEEP

I have nothing against sleep: it's just that there is a time and place for everything. If you call on me at midday I will be out like a light, or a tennis ball. I will be utterly exhausted, having spent the previous twelve hours watching meteors, touring factories, hunting fireflies, having assignations, inventing new languages, writing novels, assisting in the birth of lambs, making Faustian pacts, going to parties, night-swimming, and attending to my considerable non-electronic correspondence.

Those who speak of sleep as a 'little death' are exactly right. It's good practice for the real thing. And when it comes to the real thing, if you have practised hard enough, you will be almost off-hand. 'Nice scythe, where did you get it?'

I believe the French have the same phrase: 'la petite mort'. In their case though they use it to refer to the period immediately following sexual orgasm. How typical of them. They have forced me to mention postcoital *tristesse* on the very last page of my book.

Yes, go to sleep. Sleep is one of the great blessings of existence. It's simply that night is not the right time for it. There are so many Things to Do.